THE BOOK OF
HANDICRAFTS

THE BOOK OF
HANDICRAFTS

THE WARWICK PRESS

Acknowledgments

The publishers would like to express their grateful thanks
to the following people: Anthea Bell, for translating and
interpreting the instructions; Patience Horne, for the value
of her expert knowledge and unfailing support;
Mrs Essie Page for her invaluable advice on the knitting
and crochet patterns; to Vastiana Belfon and all those who
have helped in the preparation of this book.

Contents

Introduction 7

Flower making

Perennial piece   11

Making presents

Painted boxes   13
Enamel work   14

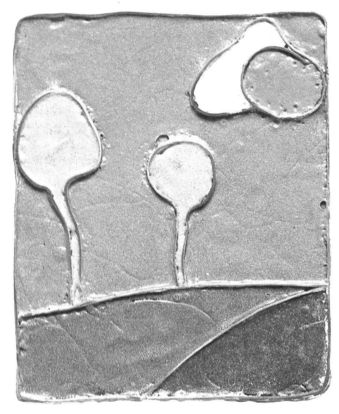

Embroidery and canvas work

Rustic tablecloth   19
A patchwork of stitches   21
Table mates   22
Vine-leaf vignette   25
Traditional embroidery   29
Rainbow letters   31
Cushions for counting   33

Weaving

Party time   37
Rustic patchwork   41

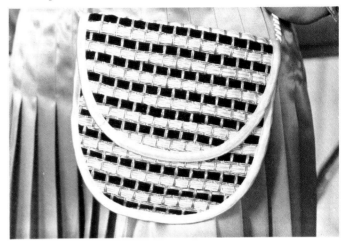

Appliqué

Farmyard fun   43

Batik magic

Material dyeing   46

Rugmaking

Warm comfort   48
Playroom magic   50
A round of colour   52
Step by step   54

Beadwork

Jewel-bright trims   56

Soft toys

Pet's corner   58
Mick the monk   66
Puppets' parade   68

Fashion and family knitting

Family gathering   72
The rugged look   74
Mother and baby team   76
Cable matchmates   78
Winter glamour   81
Partners in contrast   82
In classic style   85
Easy as winking   89
Diamonds are trumps   91
Polo-neck variations   92
The Aran look   94
Freewheeling   97
Classic simplicity   98
Fashion wraparound   99
Sporting successes   100
Sunshine set   103
Pretty as a picture   104
Cool cream   106

Fashion crochet

Follow the trend   110
Summer chic   111
Ethnic enchantment   112
Smart striping   114
Bright crochet caps   115
Cobweb finery   116
Casual contrasts   118
Summer cool   121

Crochet and knitting for the home

Curtains like Granny's   123
Old-world charm   125
Edged with lace   126
Cottage setting   128
Elegant bedspread   130

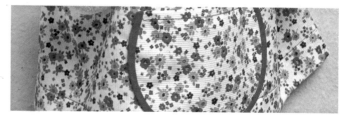

Working with cork

Coffee time   133

Working with wood

Modern setting   135

Dressmaking

In the peasant style   137
Poppet's pinafore   139
Baby's boutique   140
Beginner's piece   144
Casual elegance   147

Sewing purses and bags

Bag double-up   148
Traveller's joy   150
All set   152
Room for everything   154

Sewing with remnants

Patchwork playmates   155
Strips and stripes   157

Index   159

Introduction

THE DESIGNS IN THIS BOOK

The designs in this book are from continental collections offering an exciting selection of contents that are both interesting and worthwhile to make. Because they are continental in origin, exact equivalents in materials and colours cannot always be given, but those that are quoted are perfectly satisfactory and will achieve a result in each case which retains the intrinsic appearance of the individual design.

The wide variety of subjects included in this book gives opportunities for trying out new crafts which, apart from being fascinating and absorbing to do, can be turned to good use in the home and for fashion. Flower making gives touches of long-lasting beauty, woodwork makes modern and practical tableware, enamelling on metal produces fashionable jewellery and fabric dyeing adds the personal touch to dressmaking; this is just a selection of the features for which instructions are given.

Within the limits of such a wide range of crafts in one book, the instructions are intended as general guides, and materials, measurements, colours and so on are to be followed in an imaginative way, adapting them to individual needs and to the materials available. This collection will, therefore, be of great value and interest to craft lovers who prefer to give expression to their own creative ideas and interpretations.

KNITTING AND CROCHET HINTS

Choosing the yarn: Knitting and crochet use yarn, which is the correct term for any spun thread and the word is not descriptive of quality or type; fine baby wools, cottons, chunky mixtures, popular double knittings, are all yarns. Where a fancy texture cannot be matched exactly, the experienced knitter will know that original effects can be achieved by working different yarns together, but the required tension must, of course, be taken into consideration. For instance, two or three thicknesses of 4 ply can be mixed together, and three thicknesses of double knittings of different types can produce an attractive textured chunky look. Where an exact colour cannot be matched, choose the nearest in the range or one of personal choice.

Tension: The measurements of a design are calculated on the number of stitches and rows obtained over a given area of fabric worked in the needles and yarns being used. It is important, therefore, to check the tension by working a test square, measuring across the stitches and up the rows, before tackling the actual design.

Sizes: Many of the designs are given in two sizes, and stitches and measurements given in square brackets [] refer to the second size. Where only one set of figures is given, the instructions apply to both sizes.

Seam stitch: Continental knitting instructions often allow one extra stitch at each end of every row: this is the seam stitch (edge stitch). These are indicated in the instructions.

Metrication: Most yarns are now sold in gram balls and these come in quantities of 10, 20, 25, 50 and 100. The material quantities for knitting and crochet patterns in this book are given in total amounts. When choosing the yarns to match up with those referred to in the patterns, it is useful to remember that 28.35 gram = 1oz; 50 gram = $1\frac{3}{4}$oz.

Making up: Careful making up is essential to produce work with a professional finish. The following instructions will be helpful:

Pressing: There is such a wide range of yarns available today made from different fibres, that no standard pressing instructions can be given as some yarns should not be pressed: the ball band usually gives the instructions for the yarn in question.

For the appropriate yarns where a light pressing is required, the following hints can be used as a guide: place piece of garment on the ironing blanket, wrong side up, and pin down all around the edge, using plenty of pins, and checking measurements for size carefully. Press lightly and very carefully with a warm iron over a damp cloth, or as instructed on the ball band. Ribbed welts and borders are usually left unpressed to keep their elasticity.

Seams: Most garments are made up with a back stitch seam, which gives a neat tailored edge. This is worked as follows: place two pieces of garment together, wrong sides facing, and pin edges, matching patterns or colours very accurately. Join with a row of back stitching, worked one stitch in from the edge. For chunky yarns, a split strand or finer yarn in a toning shade can be used. For delicate garments, such as baby wear, a flat seam gives a neat smooth edge: place the two edges side by side, wrong sides up, and join ridge to ridge, with a loose oversewing stitch.

Following a chart: These are given for colour work and Fair Isle designs. On a chart, the squares represent stitches and rows. Stocking stitch is used, reading across the lines of squares for stitches (1 square = 1 stitch), and reading up the chart for rows (1 square = 1 row). Knit rows read from right to left, and purl rows from left to right, changing colour of yarn as required.

International table of needle and hook sizes

KNITTING NEEDLE			CROCHET HOOK	
USA	UK	Metric (mm)	MM Size	UK Size
00	14	2	7.00	2
0	13	$2\frac{1}{4}$	6.00	4
1	12	$2\frac{3}{4}$	5.50	5
2	11	3	5.00	6
3	10	$3\frac{1}{4}$	4.50	7
4	9	$3\frac{3}{4}$	4.00	8
5	8	4	3.50	9
6	7	$4\frac{1}{2}$	3.00	10
7	6	5		11
8	5	$5\frac{1}{2}$	2.50	12
9	4	6	2.00	13
10	3	$6\frac{1}{2}$		14
$10\frac{1}{2}$	2	7		
11	1	$7\frac{1}{2}$		
12	0	8		
13	00	9		

Knitting and crochet abbreviations

* = repeat from this sign
alt = alternate or alternately
beg = beginning
ch = chain
dc = double crochet
dec = decrease
dtr = double treble
foll = following
htr = half treble
inc = increase or increasing
K = knit
No = number
P = purl
patt = pattern
psso = pass slip stitch over
rem = remaining
rep = repeat
sks = skeins
sl st = slip stitch
st(s) = stitch(es)
st st = stocking stitch
tog = together
tr = treble
tr tr = triple treble
yf = yarn front or forward
yrn = yarn round needle

General abbreviations

cm = centimetre	g = gram(s)
m = metre	in = inch(es)
mm = millimetre	oz = ounce(s)
ft = foot or feet	yd = yard(s)

American Crochet Terminology

USA	UK
slip stitch	single crochet or slip stitch
single crochet	double crochet
half double crochet	half treble
double crochet	treble
treble crochet	double treble or long treble
double treble	triple treble

Basic knitting stitches

Stocking stitch	= 1 row knit, 1 row purl
Garter stitch	= every row knit
Reverse stocking stitch	= 1 row purl, 1 row knit
	(purl side is right side of work)

Embroidery on knitting

A quick and effective alternative to knitting-in coloured motifs is to embroider them on the knitted fabric: this is particularly suitable for small scattered motifs or where extra touches of colour are introduced into a design. The accepted stitch is Swiss Darning, also known as Knitting Stitch, as each stitch is embroidered exactly over a foundation stitch of the stocking stitch.

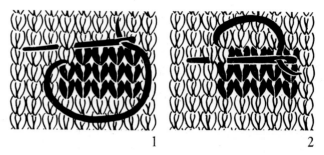

1   2

Use yarn matching the stocking-stitch fabric. Mark position of motif on right side of work. Bring needle up through centre of stitch at appropriate point from back of work, insert from right to left behind stitch immediately above (1), then down through centre of original stitch and out through centre of next stitch on left (2); thus sides of embroidery stitch cover corresponding sides of knitted stitch. The embroidery follows the knitting exactly, thus giving the stitch its name.

Rugmaking hints

Techniques: Handmade rugs are so interesting as a variety of methods can be used, all of which are surprisingly quick and easy to do. Traditional pile textures using hook methods are the most popular, but some really beautiful and unusual effects can be achieved by working embroidery stitches on rug canvas. Simple counted stitches must be used, such as cross stitch, which is both effective and practical as the crosses cover the canvas well.

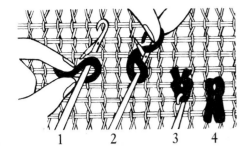

To make knot for rugmaking:
1 Place wool doubled equally on shaft of hook. Insert hook under double thread of canvas with hook turned to left. 2 Twist cut ends of loop behind the latch and across under the hook. 3 Pull hook through loop, bringing cut ends with it. 4 Give a slight tug to make knot firm.

Starting and finishing: It is usual to leave a length of unworked canvas at each short end of the rug piece, to be turned to the back of the rug and stitched down, or faced with rug binding on the underside. The design is usually worked right up to the long sides (selvedges) of the canvas, and the selvedge is turned under and hemmed down or covered with a crossed over stitch. To work this binding stitch, the principle is to oversew, going forwards and backwards so that the threads are crossed as follows: with wrong side of rug facing, darn in yarn, go over edge to 3rd or 4th hole, back to 1st, over to 4th or 5th, back to 2nd, and so on. This double stitch covers the selvedge well and is hard-wearing.

Embroidery notes

Working hints: The two most popular forms of embroidery are the free-stitch method, using well-loved stitches such as satin, stem and chain (or loop) stitches and counted embroidery. The free-stitch method uses stitches worked on linen in outline, or to fill the motifs on floral designs and sprays or for larger pieces such as screens and panels. The nature of this embroidery allows for greater freedom of interpretation by the worker. A life-size outline of the motif to be worked is given, which is traced and transferred to the material. Hints on how to copy and transfer a motif are given below.

Counted embroidery is simpler to do and is recommended for the beginner. Symmetrical stitches, such as cross stitch, are used, working on fabric in which the threads are regular and can be counted, thus each stitch is 'worked by the counted thread'. A chart of the design is given, with each square representing a stitch over the appropriate number of threads. With practice, beautiful and historical stitches, such as Holbein, can be introduced to produce more elaborate and varied effects.

Tracing and transferring a motif: It is a simple matter to copy a motif to give an image which can then be transferred to a fabric for embroidery. First take a tracing of the motif using ordinary tracing paper. Mark position of motif on the fabric. Place a piece of carbon paper between drawing and fabric, and lightly draw over the outline of the motif so that an image is pressed on to the fabric; do this very gently so that the carbon does not smudge the fabric (worn carbon can be used or it is possible to obtain dressmaker's carbon paper).

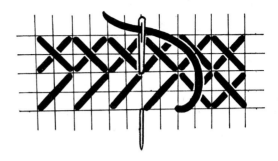

To work simple counted cross stitch:
Counted cross stitch can be worked over any evenly woven fabric or canvas, using yarns from the finest embroidery threads to thick rug wools.

The stitches should be worked in two rows – a row of starting stitches in one direction and these are crossed on the return row: diagram shows the second row in work. It is essential that the top stitches all lie in the same direction, since otherwise the work looks ragged and uneven.

Finishing touches: A piece of handworked embroidery deserves special attention to the finishing. First do any neatening that is required; trim raw edges, remove basting stitches, trim or tidy any short ends or loose threads (the wrong side of the work should look almost as neat as the right side).

Pressing: The degree of pressing relates to the type of embroidery fabric used. Place work face downwards on a soft ironing blanket, pat into shape, pinning if necessary, and press very carefully over a damp cloth; start with a warm iron and increase heat gently, taking care that the iron does not get too hot.

Seams and hems should be stitched as invisibly as possible, and mitred corners on articles such as tablecloths and mats, given a professional finish. Finished articles should be given a final pressing as before.

Dressmaking and soft toys

These require paper patterns, which are given in the instructions in the form of graph-paper plans. These must be drawn up and enlarged to form a paper pattern for cutting out as described here.

To make a paper pattern: The instructions give cutting layouts and pattern plans (all measurements are given in centimetres only). As the plans are reduced in size, they must be copied by drawing and scaling up to the actual measurements, on strong paper such as brown packing paper. Mark out paper in squares to correspond with plan. Then carefully copy the outlines of the pieces as you draw. When the pieces have all been copied, you have a paper pattern from which the shapes can be cut out and pinned on the fabric.

Flower making

Perennial piece

This 'flower arrangement' captures the beauty of real flowers. It is made of pine and larch cones and cotton-wool balls.

   If you like experimenting – doing things with your hands and using your imagination – you will enjoy making this flower arrangement. It takes a little time and trouble, but in the end you have a bunch of flowers that will never fade.

Working instructions:

You need a basket or bowl, which can be earthenware or brass; the latter must be given a thin coating of lacquer to prevent oxydization. Fill the bowl with layers of plastic foam cut exactly to size (picture 1) and stick in place with adhesive at the edge. Paint surface of top layer a dark colour (see picture 6). For the flowers, you will need dried pine cones. Cut them in half with a pair of pincers (picture 2). The broader bottom half of the cone is used to make a flower. Make a hole in base of cone, insert a skewer, stained to colour, and glue in place to form flower stalk.

Dip the flowers in thinned-down white liquid dye and let them dry well. Repeat the process, using coloured dyes, either plain or mixed depending on the colours you want (picture 3). If a cone shows a tendency to close up after being dyed, put it in the oven to dry out until it opens up again. Spread adhesive in the flower centres and scatter them with grains of millet, or paint centres in a contrasting colour. The arrangement will look particularly lifelike if some of the flowers are given a shiny appearance by spraying them with a clear lacquer (picture 4).

For the rest of the arrangement, you can use poppy capsules, dried grasses and thistle heads. Larch cones, either coloured or left natural brown, are particularly suitable: snipped apart and coloured pink or dark red, they look like pompon roses. Another idea is to glue small cotton-wool balls to skewers, colour and lacquer them and decorate by sticking on small acorns or cloves; or they can be dipped into poppy or mustard seeds (see picture 5). Another idea is to halve larger cotton-wool balls and cover them with dried peas, or roll them into an oval shape, apply glue and turn them around in oats, finally dipping into coloured dye.

Add green foliage or sprays of dark red berries to this colourful flower arrangement, and if you would like to give the whole thing a touch of fragrance add statice, which lasts a long time and will not drop.

Arrange 'flowers' from centre of bowl outwards, making sure the colours set each other off well. Intersperse with foliage and berries. Do not crowd the flowers, but space them openly as in the picture – they will look more natural.

1 Cutting layers of plastic foam.
2 Cutting pine cones.
3 Dipping 'flowers' in coloured dyes.
4 Spraying with clear lacquer.
5 Materials for decorating cotton-wool balls.
6 Arranging flowers in bowl.

Motif for round box, full size.
Trace it on to cardboard.

Making presents

Painted boxes

Decorating chip boxes like these is a form of handicraft where individual taste and original ideas can be expressed. With imagination and delicacy of touch, you can create something really new.

The technique, though not difficult, requires practice, and you should experiment before actually starting work, as it is difficult to be precise about quantities of materials and paint for the mixtures. There are two possible methods of working: the first, described below, is for the two oval boxes shown opposite full size; the second is shown in the sequence of pictures at the foot of this page.

OVAL BOXES: METHOD 1
Materials:
Powdered chalk, plastic wood, primer, poster paints, 2 oval chip boxes, clear lacquer, medium and fine paintbrushes.

Working instructions:
First paint box with primer and let it dry. While it is drying, trace outlines of motifs from these pictures and transfer them to boxes.

Next make a mixture of chalk and plastic wood; experiment with this mixture, which should be thick and firm enough to mould shapes in relief. When it is the right consistency, apply it to those areas which are to stand out in relief, such as flowers, leaves, stems, and so on.

Apply mixture in several coats, graduating according to the desired thickness of the finished motif. If the mixture becomes too stiff, it can be thinned down with water. Indentations can be made on the motifs with the handle of the paintbrush, to add to the three-dimensional effect. Let motifs dry thoroughly. Now paint them with poster paints, varying colours as illustrated, and then using the fine brush to paint in details such as small leaves, buds and flower calyxes. Finally paint entire surface of box around motifs with background colour. Spray or paint over finished box with clear lacquer, to make the surface more durable.

ROUND BOX: METHOD 2
The materials needed to decorate the round chip box: powdered chalk, plastic wood, primer, poster paints, clear lacquer, medium and thin paintbrushes.

1 First paint box with primer and leave to dry. Prepare cardboard template tracing of full-size flower motif opposite. Transfer 5 motifs to form garland round top of box.

2 Mix chalk and plastic wood; the consistency should be thick enough to mould shapes. Add paint in desired colours to mixture and paint mixture on to those parts of the design which are to stand out in relief.

3 After motifs have dried, paint carefully all round them with background colour, adding small details with the fine brush at this stage.

4 Spray or paint entire surface of box with clear lacquer.

Enamel work

If you have ever worked with enamel you will know what lovely effects can be achieved. The technique given here is particularly simple, and you will enjoy trying it. Start with a single shape, such as the oval pendant (pictures 1–5).

1 Here are the materials and tools needed for enamelling. Materials are listed for each piece of jewelry.
2 Cut an oval to desired size from sheet brass, using scissors or craft shears.
3 Powdered colour is scattered straight on to metal oval from small containers.
4 Now the colour is baked on; lay a piece of foil between the kiln and the oval itself.
5 Rub metal oval with sandpaper after baking, to produce a dulled surface effect.
6 For a different effect, colours can be painted on a baked metal shape using powdered colour mixed with fat oil. This gives a shiny finish, as in the butterfly brooch.
7 For decoration in relief, copper wire is bent, stuck into place with adhesive and then baked as in the landscape scene.
8 After baking on the wire, powdered colour can be applied to separate parts of design.
9 Finally bake on the kiln again, placing foil under metal.

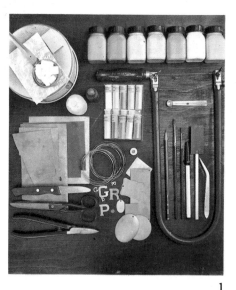

1

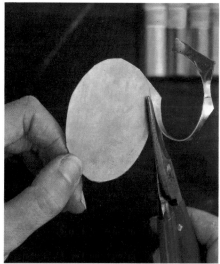

2

3

4

5

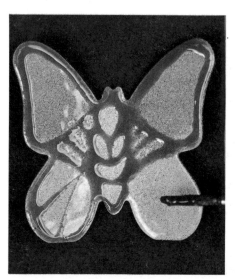

6

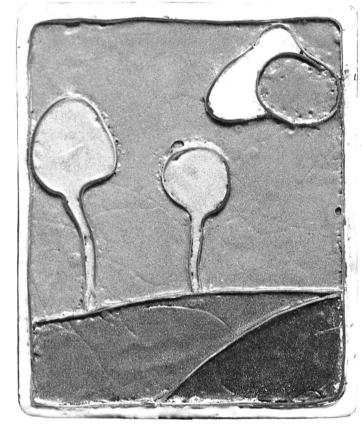

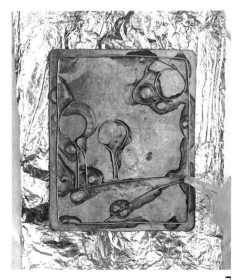

7

8

9

10

11

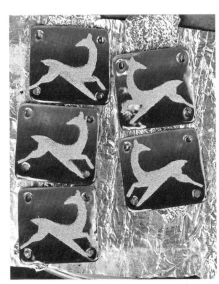

12   13

The four illustrations above show clearly the stages in the making of the bracelet, from the life-size deer motif to the finished individual links, where three of the motifs have been reversed.

PENDANT (Pictures 1–5, page 14)
Materials:
Small kiln able to reach a temperature of 180°C (356°F); special fuel for kiln; pots or containers of powdered colour with mesh over the top; sheet copper or sheet brass, or ready-stamped metal shapes; craft shears, scissors or fret-saw; sandpaper; pencils; brush.

Working instructions:
Pictures 1–5 show the basic principles of this technique. Choose a shape, draw it on sheet brass and cut out with an old pair of scissors or craft shears (or there are many pre-stamped metal shapes available). Smooth edges with sand-paper, and remove any traces of grease from the surface with detergent. Mix powdered colour to achieve desired shade and sprinkle it on the oval through a small sieve with a fine mesh (or use unmixed powdered colour straight from sprinkler containers). Lay oval on a piece of foil, placing this on kiln and bake at a temperature of about 150–180°C (300–356°F). Quarter of a piece of special fuel will heat kiln to about 150°C (300°F). After baking, oval can be rubbed with sandpaper to produce a dulled surface effect.

BUTTERFLY BROOCH (Picture 6, page 14)
Materials:
As for oval pendant, plus fat oil.
This picture shows a shape which has already been coloured plain and baked. The design is now painted on the baked surface. Mix powdered colour with fat oil and use like liquid paint. After painting, let surface dry for 2–3 hours, then bake. However, instead of baking, simply leave the shape to dry for several days.

COPPER-WIRE PICTURE (Pictures 7–9, page 15)
Materials:
As for oval pendant, plus copper wire, pincers, adhesive.
For this landscape scene, shapes are formed from bent copper wire and placed on a piece of sheet copper cut to size. Apply adhesive, bake at 150°C (300°F) until surface is dry. Fill shapes with powdered colour, bake again. As powdered colour melts, more powder can be applied to the shapes.

BRACELET (Pictures 10–13)
Materials:
As for oval pendant, plus transparent paper.
Choose a simple design (or copy deer motif), lay transparent paper over it and trace; the paper can be held down with sellotape at the edges. Cut out shape of design with scissors or knife. Now place paper with its cut-out centre on a piece of metal which has already been coloured plain and baked, and sprinkle whole area thickly with colour. Lift off paper very carefully and finally bake metal. The metal shapes can be joined with strips of leather or cord.

PENDANT (Pictures 14 and 15)
You can make all sorts of different pieces of jewelry with this enamelling technique. Here is a pretty pendant made of three links.

Picture 14 shows the finished pendant. After covering a metal surface with light-coloured powdered colour and baking it, cool and then draw a design on the surface in dark felt pen. Sprinkle light powdered colour over the metal again and bake; the design will remain visible. Join metal shapes with leather or cord.

BELT DECORATION (Picture 16)
Materials:
As for oval pendant, plus copper or brass wire, solder, soldering iron. Draw shape of belt buckle and cut out with fretsaw. Copper or brass wire is shaped to the basic form of buckle and soldered in place. Remove excess solder with a sharp knife. The other pieces of the belt are shaped with wire, and shaped areas are filled with powdered colour and baked; cool and repeat process. A final smoothing of the buckle with sandpaper will expose the strap.

Points to note:
Fat oil and suitable adhesive can be obtained from any craft shop dealing in enamelling materials.
1 If the kiln gets too hot, the molten powder will boil, develop blisters, and the colour will peel off later.
2 The baked enamel surface is liable to be damaged by a hard knock or scratching with any sharp object.
3 The powdered colour may run if several, mixed with fat oil, are to be used together, so it is best to bake each colour on separately.
4 After baking let the metal cool as slowly as possible, as the surface cracks easily.
5 Copper wire bent to shape, coated with adhesive and baked on must lie quite flat on the metal, or the shapes will easily come loose later.

14

Pictures 14 and 15 illustrate the pendant. The small picture shows the graduating shapes of the links onto which the connecting design is being coloured. In the large illustration, the model shows how charming the finished pendant looks when worn.
Picture 16: the belt has been wound round the hand to show off the attractive blue-and-white motif of links and buckle.

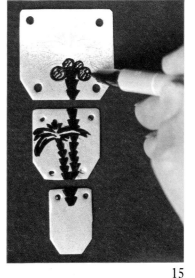

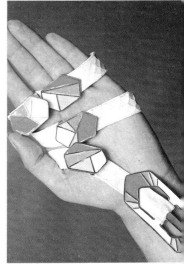

15   16

Embroidery and canvas work

Rustic tablecloth

A pretty cloth makes your table look particularly appetizing, and adds to the pleasure of mealtimes. The rustic-style cloth pictured here has a broad cross-stitch border in a traditional design worked all round the edge.

You could equally well use the pattern on a table runner, or embroider it on cushions for your dining area. The simple, repeating design is easily adaptable for the central strip of a long refectory tablecloth, and the small diamonds could be picked out and worked on matching table napkins.

Size:
136 × 136cm (53 × 53in).

Materials:
Tapestry yarn: 34 sks cream, 6 sks rust. Fabric for cloth must have a weave with threads which are easy to count; you will need 140cm (1½yd) of fabric 140cm (54in) wide, with approximately 14 threads to 2.5cm (1in).

Measurements for stitching:
54 threads of weave = 18 cross stitches = 10cm (4in).

Design chart:
Chart shows corner, connecting section of the design, and pattern repeat, plus line to complete design. Each cross = 1 cross stitch worked over 3 threads of the weave. Blank squares = unembroidered fabric.

Working instructions:
Trim raw edges of fabric. Start with corner section 10cm (4in) in from the edge, then work connecting section, 6 repeats and last stitch. Next work connecting section followed by corner section = 217 cross stitches in all. Work all 4 sides in the same way. For inner rectangle, count 75 threads in from top of border, and work cross stitch in cream over next 3 threads all the way round.

Making up:
Stitch a narrow hem round the edge.

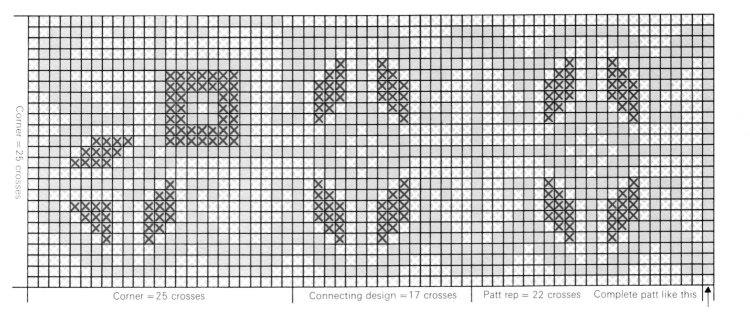

Corner = 25 crosses

Corner = 25 crosses   Connecting design = 17 crosses   Patt rep = 22 crosses   Complete patt like this

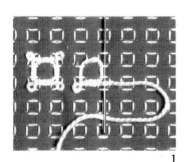

1

2

3

4

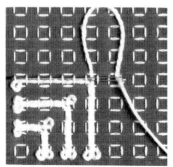

5

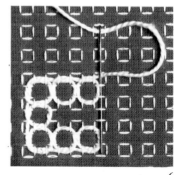

6

A patchwork of stitches

Pattern threading is quick and easy and simple enough even for children's hands. The original cloth was worked on a blue huckaback fabric with a surface pattern of small white squares; the white cotton is darned through the loose white threads of the squares. Any counted fabric with raised lines or squares suitable for darning would do. You can follow the examples given here, or make up patterns of your own.

Size:
153cm × 153cm (60in × 60in).

Materials:
Anchor Stranded Cotton, 40 sks in white (use full strand). Blue huckaback fabric with surface threads in white, 155cm (60in) of fabric 155cm (60in) wide, or suitable fabric.

Method:
Pattern threading: the cotton is passed under the surface threads. Each pattern square is worked over a set of 12 squares horizontally and vertically (144 squares in all).

Working instructions:
Decide on the number of squares to be worked in centre of fabric; a plain border of unworked fabric can be left round the edge. When embroidery is finished, turn hem round the edge, mitring corners, or face with white binding.

Pattern 1: Each pattern square consists of 16 small checks. Work each design over 2 squares horizontally and 2 squares vertically (4 in all). Bring up needle in bottom left corner and thread cotton once round the 4 squares. On next round, loop cotton round outer corners of the squares as shown.

Pattern 2: Each pattern square consists of 9 diagonal blocks. Work each design over a set of 4 squares horizontally and vertically (16 in all). Thread cotton diagonally through the squares. When repeating pattern, change direction of the threading to give variety (see illustration of completed cloth).

Pattern 3: Each pattern square consists of 12 straight lines. 2 straight rows worked horizontally over the desired number of squares (working picture shows a shortened version of the pattern). Bring needle up through the first square, *thread cotton round 2 corner surface threads of square, pass under vertical surface threads to the last square, turn by passing needle under the horizontal surface threads of this square and

the cotton thread, and work return journey in the same way. On reaching first square, pass cotton around 2 remaining corner surface threads and take needle down through the middle of the square; bring needle up again 1 square above, repeat from *.

Pattern 4: Each pattern square consists of 9 flower motifs. First work the horizontal rows. Bring needle up in space between 2 squares, *take cotton 1 square further on (starting thread), then pass it once round and under surface threads of the 4 squares, to form 4 loops as shown, and under the starting thread. Repeat from *, moving 1 space further on each time. Work vertical rows to match.

Pattern 5: Each pattern square consists of 4 right-angled blocks. As for Pattern 3, but working in right angles for 5 rows towards the centre. Work 5 rows thus. Work 3 repeats of this design to fill motif, as shown in illustration of cloth.

Pattern 6: Each pattern square consists of 9 small checks. Work each check over 4 squares horizontally and vertically (16 in all). Bring needle up in corner square and thread around surface threads of 4 squares as shown until pattern is complete.

Pattern 7: Each pattern square consists of 4 rows of loops. Work loops to and fro over sets of 3 squares in a horizontal line. Bring needle up just below bottom surface thread of square, pass thread under square, *then work 1 loop round corner surface threads of next squares to the right as shown, return to beginning of loop and pass needle under surface threads of square above, repeat from *. To turn after last row, take needle through to back of work and bring up again close to same place. Work return journey to form loops in the other direction.

Pattern 8: Each pattern square consists of rows of alternating loops. Work as for Pattern 6, working in rows round 4 sides towards centre, but leaving corner surface threads of 2 squares free between the edges. Alternate motifs on each round.

Pattern 9: Each pattern square consists of 16 daisy motifs. First thread horizontal rows. Bring needle up to side of square, thread cotton 2 squares further on, *thread round corner surface threads of right-hand square on row above, under horizontal surface threads of the middle square and the cotton, round corner surface threads of left-hand square on row below, under the 2 vertical surface threads of the middle square, passing over the cotton, move on 3 squares and repeat from *. Work vertical rows to match.

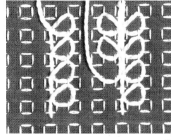

7

8

9

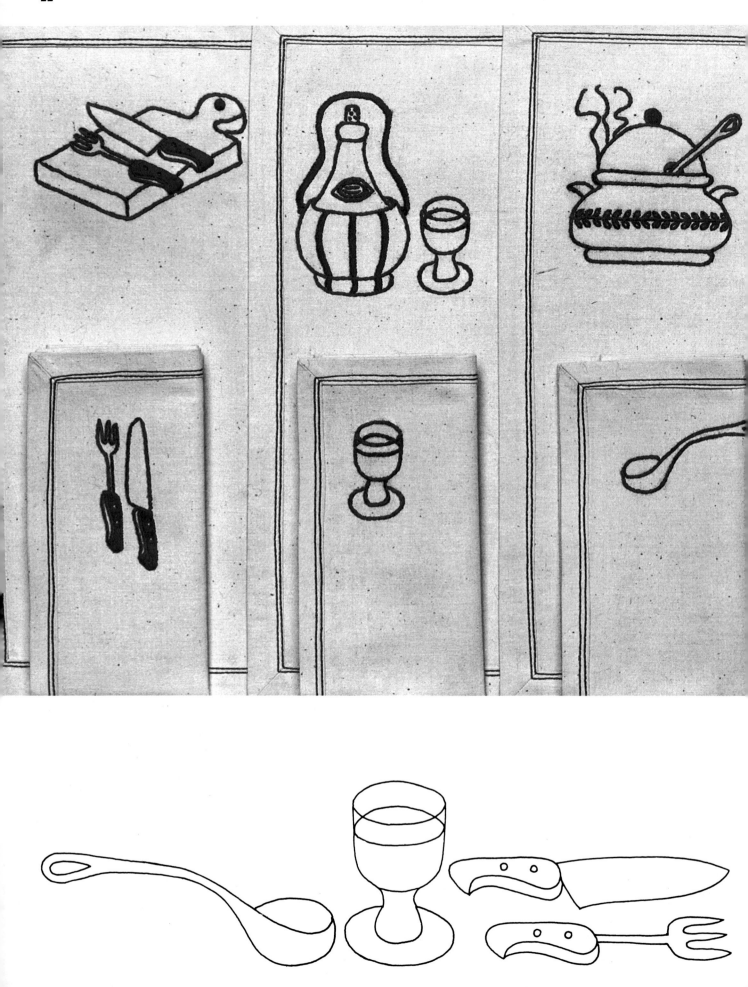

Table mates

Nothing could be simpler to copy than these
cheerful motifs, inspired by the friendly everyday
objects to be found in the kitchen. The charm lies in
the informality of the motifs, which are embroidered
fairly freely to add to their rustic appearance.

Three examples of place settings are illustrated,
with the napkin motifs echoing the larger designs on
the place mats. Work as many sets as you need,
ringing the changes on the motifs – and why not
scatter them over a matching supper cloth?

A quick alternative to the embroidered hemlines
would be to bind round the edges with matching
binding.

Materials:
Suitable material, such as linen or calico.
Anchor Stranded Cotton for the embroidery.

Working instructions:
Cut out fabric for place mats and napkins as required. Trace
and transfer full-size motifs (opposite and below) as described on page 9, positioning on the fabric as illustrated.
Embroider with stem, satin and loop stitches and French
knots, using 3 strands for finer outlines and 4 strands for
thicker fillings.
Press embroidery (see page 9), turn hems round mats and
napkins and mitre corners. Decorate hems with 2 rows of
stem or back stitch in 2 strands of cotton.

Vine-leaf vignette

Embroidered in cool green shades, this pretty design makes an inviting tablecloth. It is simple to make, in satin stitch and stem stitch.

The life-size motifs on pages 26–7 are copied and arranged on the linen in garlands as illustrated – a smaller rectangle in the centre and a larger one on the outside; the close-up illustration below shows how the motifs link up at the corner.

If you want to work a smaller cloth, arrange a medium-sized rectangle in the centre of a 91cm (36in) or 140cm (54in) square of linen. For matching table mats, embroider single leaves in the corners.

Size:
130 × 175cm (50 × 70in).

Materials:
24 sks Coats Anchor Stranded Cotton: 10 sks mid-green, 6 sks dark green, 8 sks brown. Piece of embroidery linen 140 × 185cm (56 × 72in) wide.

Stitches:
1 *Satin stitch*, using 3 strands of cotton. 2 *Stem stitch*, using 4 strands of cotton for outlines of leaves, 3 strands for stems, 2 strands for veins of leaves.

Working instructions:
Life-size outlines of motifs are given overleaf. Trace and transfer to fabric as described on page 9. Mark exact centre of the linen. Around this point mark out with tacking stitches 1 rectangle 30 × 52cm (12 × 20½in) for centre design, then 1 rectangle 73.6 × 117cm (29 × 45in), outside this for the outer border. Trace sprays of motif for larger rectangle as follows. Starting at top right corner, position and transfer corner design, then transfer the small design 3 times along long side of rectangle; join to shorter side of corner design. Transfer corner design. For narrow side, trace the small design. Transfer motifs round other side to complete border all round the edge.

Next transfer designs for smaller rectangle. Beginning at top right corner again, transfer corner design. Then cut short side of corner design, including corner leaf, from the tracing, and transfer on long side of rectangle, joining it to corner design. Now transfer corner design at right angles to corner leaf. Complete rectangle by transferring short side of corner design including corner leaf.

Work outlines of leaves in stem stitch in mid green, and veins of leaves and stems in dark green. Work bunches of grapes and thick tendrils in satin stitch in brown.

Turn under edges of tablecloth and tack, and mitre corners at the same time; stitch round hem by hand.

VINE-LEAF GARLANDS
Life-size motifs for tracing for embroidered
tablecloth on page 24

Traditional embroidery

The designs on this tablecloth are worked centrally, but you could arrange them over the entire cloth, or work them as a border. Choose an evenly woven fabric for the cloth, so that you can count the threads easily.

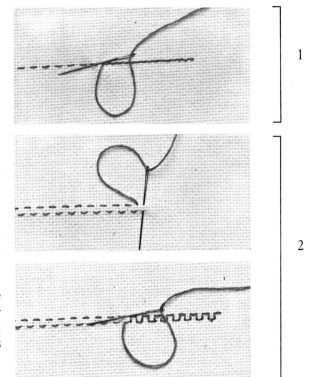

1

2

Holbein stitch:
Holbein or double running stitch consists of running stitch worked on both sides of the fabric. The name comes from old paintings, particularly those of the two Holbeins, where the clothes of the sitters show designs in this type of embroidery. Here are two of the main ways of working the stitch.
1 *Straight line:* work running stitch in one direction, then back along the same line in the other direction, so as to form an unbroken line. Always take up the same number of threads in the weave of the fabric. If working diagonal lines, take up the same number of crossing threads in the weave each time.
2 *Squared line:* work two parallel lines of running stitch on the first journey, bringing the needle vertically through the fabric between the rows as shown. Take up the same number of threads each time. On the way back, work the vertical stitches to form a squared line as shown, joining the gaps between stitches on the top row with horizontal stitches. The work should look exactly the same on both sides.

Materials:
8 skeins Coats Anchor Stranded Cotton: 3 sks rust, 2 sks each black and green, 1 sk yellow. Piece of ivory or natural linen or suitable fabric for counted embroidery, with approximately 18–20 threads to 2.5cm (1in), 140cm (54in) wide.

Stitches:
Work cross stitch and Holbein stitch (see separate instructions and pictures) with 3 strands of cotton, working to squares formed by 2 threads of weave in each direction.

Design charts:
Chart A shows a quarter of the pattern of large diamond motif; complete by matching the other three quarters to fit. The small motif is given in full in chart B. Each cross = 1 cross stitch; strokes = Holbein stitch. Work colours as shown on charts. Blank squares each = 2 threads of fabric weave in each direction.

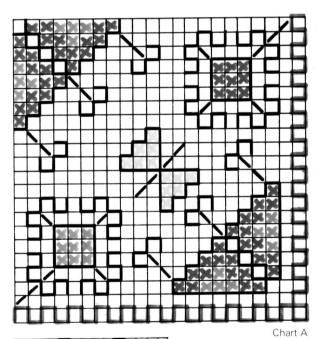

Chart A

Working instructions:
Work large diamond from centre outwards. Centre threads are marked on chart A. First work cross-stitch central section of the design, then work the Holbein stitches. Work surrounding parts of the design, and finally the outer border. Work smaller motif in the same way, working first the cross stitch and then the Holbein stitch.

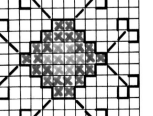

Chart B

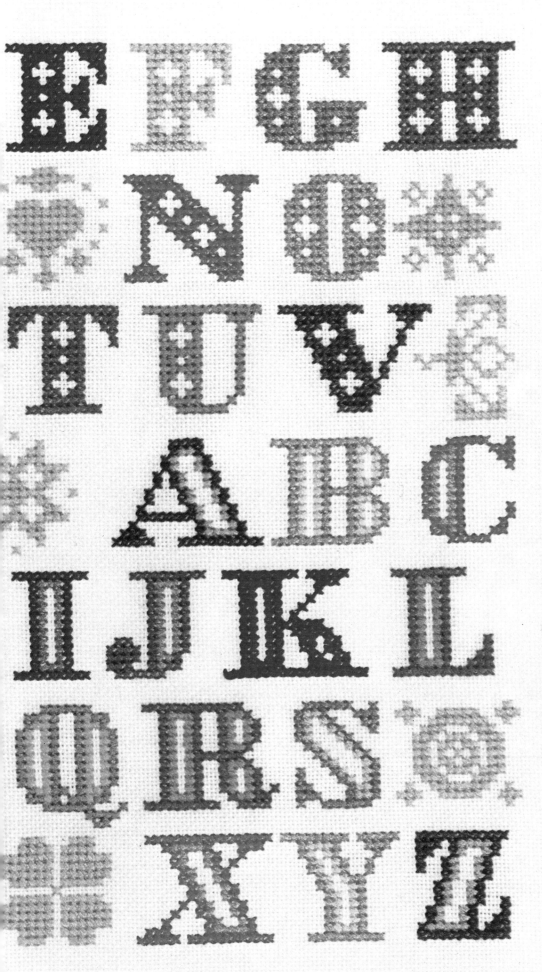

Rainbow letters

A brilliant display of letters in all the colours of the rainbow. These two alphabets give you a choice of designs: the top working shows the cross-stitch fillings worked to leave open threads in a pretty star design, and below, the letters are outlined with rows of stitches in shaded colours. Scattered throughout is a selection of small motifs that can be introduced for extra decorative touches.

The first alphabet has a quaint, old-fashioned air, and these letters, together with the little motifs, could make up a charming Victorian sampler. In contrast, the second alphabet follows the contemporary trend to give boldly bright, simple touches to home accessories.

The alphabets are worked in counted cross stitch and the size of the letters can be adjusted as required by altering the scale of the materials, working in 3 or less strands on fine material, or with more strands on coarser fabric. Work to a fine scale for more delicate articles, such as embroidering your own monogram on to personal linens, or on a bib or other nursery items. Bolder, more colourful touches call for a coarser scale, for playroom and kitchen pieces, such as cushions, toy-bag, holdall, gardening apron and so on. Basic instructions for simple cross stitch are given on page 9.

Cushions for counting

These cushions are rather special: not just for sitting on, not just for throwing around the room – children can use them to learn to count. They are amusing and colourful, too, and will be an asset to any nursery. Charts are given for 9 designs, so make your choice.

The cushions are very easy to work – child's play in every sense of the word, since even children could try making them. All you need is a suitable background canvas, or counted-thread fabric, in width about 50cm (20in). Tapestry yarn is used for the embroidery.

Working instructions:
The method is very simple. Flat stitches are oversewn into the squares of the woven backing material as shown in close-up illustration of working stitch. 2 stitches form one square. This means that each square on the colour pattern chart represents 2 stitches side by side in the same colour.

Making up:
When you have finished the front of the cushion it is sewn to the back, cut from stout cotton material; cut the fabric about 2cm ($\frac{3}{4}$in) larger all round than the embroidered front. Make little darts about 0.5cm (just under $\frac{1}{4}$in) wide at each corner, each dart 10cm (4in) long. Place two parts of cushion cover right sides together, baste and stitch, leaving an opening at the lower edge for the filling. Sew up the opening with invisible stitches after filling the cushion.

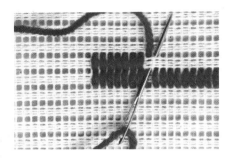

Working close-up of the stitch, showing the upright stitches worked into the holes of the canvas in even rows. The stitches can be varied by working over 2 or more threads to cover the ground more rapidly and give a bolder effect; remember that this method would mean allowing 2 squares of the chart to each stitch.

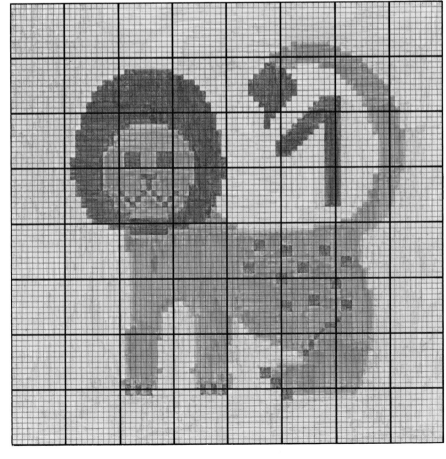

Cushion 1

Green: 9 sks

Orange: 4 sks

Brown: 2 sks

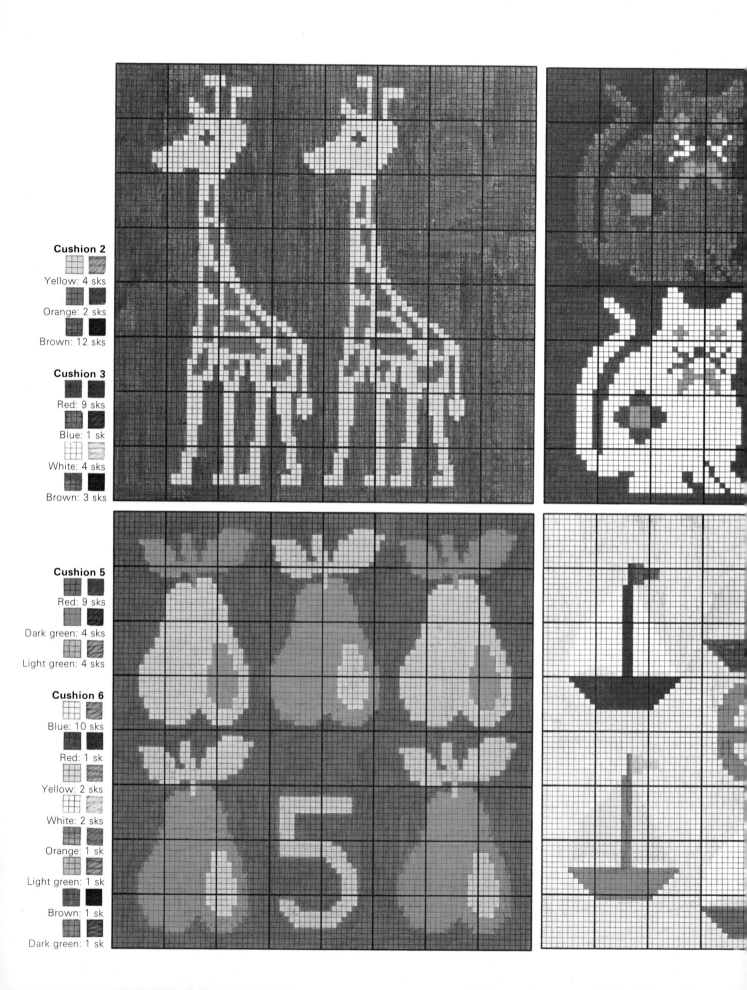

Cushion 2

Yellow: 4 sks

Orange: 2 sks

Brown: 12 sks

Cushion 3

Red: 9 sks

Blue: 1 sk

White: 4 sks

Brown: 3 sks

Cushion 5

Red: 9 sks

Dark green: 4 sks

Light green: 4 sks

Cushion 6

Blue: 10 sks

Red: 1 sk

Yellow: 2 sks

White: 2 sks

Orange: 1 sk

Light green: 1 sk

Brown: 1 sk

Dark green: 1 sk

Cushion 4

Yellow: 9 sks

Dark green: 2 sks

Light green: 2 sks

Red: 2 sks

Orange: 2 sks

Cushion 7

Dark green: 8 sks

Brown: 2 sks

Plum: 1 sk

Red: 2 sks

Orange: 2 sks

Yellow: 2 sks

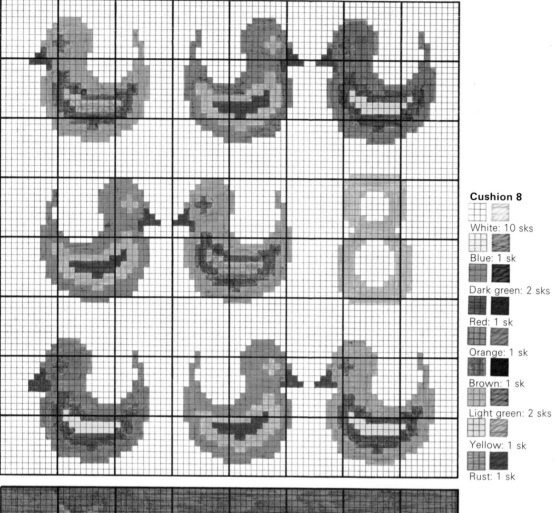

Cushion 8

White: 10 sks

Blue: 1 sk

Dark green: 2 sks

Red: 1 sk

Orange: 1 sk

Brown: 1 sk

Light green: 2 sks

Yellow: 1 sk

Rust: 1 sk

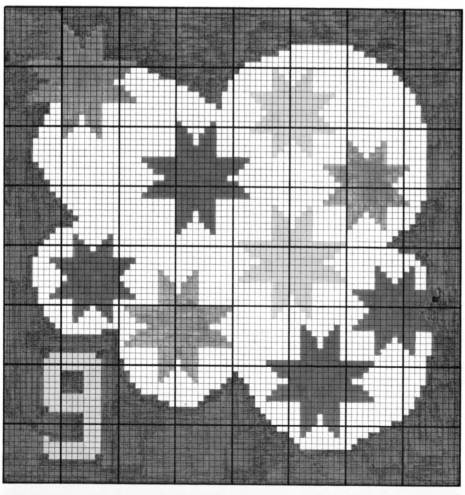

Cushion 9

Blue: 5 sks

White: 6 sks

Orange: 2 sks

Red: 2 sks

Yellow: 1 sk

Weaving

Party time

These evening bags are quick to make as the shapes are so simple. The basic principle is an uncomplicated weaving technique formed by threading lengths of braid or other suitable material through an easily made weaving frame. Instructions are given for four different shapes and colour combinations.

See page 9 for instructions on scaling up plans.

Read the following instructions for the weaving technique first, as they apply to all four bags.

Weaving instructions:

This type of weaving needs a frame which is easily made. Take stout cardboard (wood-pulp board) and cut it 3cm (1in) larger all round than you want your finished piece of weaving. Measurements are given in the instructions for each bag and plan.

1 Wind braid into a ball. Cut warp (lengthwise) and weft (across) threads to lengths given for each bag.

2 Make notches with scissors in the two narrow sides of frame about 12mm ($\frac{1}{2}$in) deep, at intervals of about 8mm. Insert warp threads into these notches and stick the ends down by overlaying them with adhesive tape at back of frame.

3 Warp threads are now stretched across frame from the two sets of notches. Weave weft threads across them, leaving ends free at both sides. Thread weft threads alternately over and under the warp as in ordinary darning. After weaving is finished, stick down the ends of both warp and weft threads with sellotape at front of frame. Then remove frame by cutting through extreme ends of warp threads all round the work along the outer edge of the sellotape.

4 Machine-stitch outer edges firmly, using zig-zag stitch. To prevent the work fraying, the strips of sellotape must lie on the underside of the work. Cut all loose ends close to seam.

EVENING POUCH

Materials:

Wood-pulp board, 25 × 57cm (10 × 22$\frac{1}{2}$in). Narrow braid: 34m (37yd) in silver, 16m (17$\frac{1}{2}$yd) in dark blue, 15m (16$\frac{1}{2}$yd) in white. 1.20m (1$\frac{1}{4}$yd) white silky-textured bias binding (or ribbon) 3cm (1in) wide. 1.20m (1$\frac{1}{4}$yd) white cord. *Lining material:* 25 × 55cm (10 × 26in). Strong adhesive tape. Sellotape.

Using plan as a guide, draw up 2 pattern pieces to their full sizes. Part 1 = the entire oval. Part 2 = section marked by arrow.

Working instructions:

Cut 27 notches in each of the narrow sides of wood-pulp board. Cut braid to following lengths: 27 warp threads in silver each 63cm (24$\frac{3}{4}$in) long, 53 weft threads in dark blue 30cm (12in) long, 50 weft threads in silver 30cm (12in) long, 50 weft threads in white 30cm (12in) long. Work weft as follows: *1st row:* 1 thread silver, 2 parallel threads blue. *2nd row:* 1 thread silver. *3rd row:* 2 threads white. Repeat from * as required for measurement of finished woven material.

Lay the 2 pattern pieces on the completed woven material. Draw round the shapes to give outline of bag and flap.

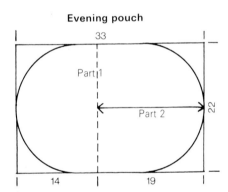

Evening pouch

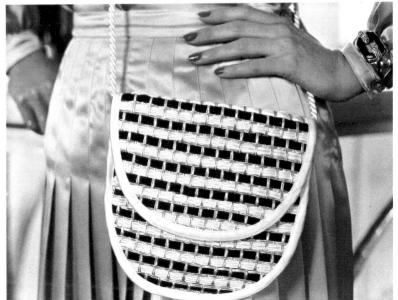

1

3

4

Remove pattern and secure outline by sticking sellotape round the edge; stitch down with zig-zag stitch.

Cut lining for both parts of bag; baste bag and lining together, wrong sides facing, then stitch outer edges together. Bind top edge of Part 2 of bag with binding to a depth of 1cm (just under ½in). Then place both parts of bag together, wrong sides facing, and baste edges. Bind round edges of entire oval of bag with binding and turn flap over. Sew on cord for shoulder strap.

SHOULDER BAG
Materials:
Wood-pulp board, 45 × 22cm (17¾ × 8½in); cardboard for stiffening, 17 × 14cm (6½ × 5½in). Narrow braid: 42m (46yd) in silver, 11m (12yd) in dark blue. 1m (1yd) dark blue corded ribbon 2.5cm (1in) wide. 1m (1yd) silver-grey cord. *Lining material:* 45 × 25cm (17¾ × 10in). Strong adhesive tape. Sellotape.

Working instructions:
Cut 25 notches in the 2 narrow sides of wood-pulp board. Cut braid to following lengths: 20 warp threads 55cm (21½in) long in silver, 5 warp threads 55cm (21½in) long in dark blue, 120 weft threads 25cm (10in) long in silver, 23 weft threads 25cm (10in) long in dark blue.
Fix warp threads in place as follows: 4 threads silver, *1 thread blue, 3 threads silver. Repeat from * 3 times. End with 1 thread blue, 4 threads silver.
Work weft threads as follows: *4 rows silver, 1 row dark blue, repeat from * to end. Tape down and stitch outer edges.
Cut bag lining to same size as bag, place them wrong sides together and baste, stitching outer edges together; at the same time insert piece of cardboard, cut to size, in lower part of bag to stiffen it. Trim lower edge with corded ribbon to a depth of 1cm (just under ½in). Fold lower part of bag upwards, matching x to o (see plan). Baste sides together and trim bag all round with corded ribbon. Fold over flap. Sew on cord for shoulder strap.

POCHETTE
Materials:
Wood-pulp board; 48 × 23cm (19 × 9in). Narrow braid: 25m (27½yd) in yellow, 25m (27½yd) in black. *Lining material:* 25 × 50cm (10 × 20in). 1.10m (1¼yd) black silky-textured bias binding 3cm (1in) wide. Strong adhesive tape. Sellotape.

Working instructions:
Cut 25 notches in each of the narrow sides of wood-pulp board. Cut braid to following lengths: 13 warp threads 53cm (21in) long in black, 12 warp threads 53cm (21in) long in yellow, 67 weft threads 28cm (11in) long in black, 67 weft threads 28cm (11in) long in yellow.
Fix warp threads in place as follows: 2 threads black, *3 threads yellow, 3 threads black. Repeat from * twice. End with 3 threads yellow and 2 threads black.
Work weft threads as follows: *6 rows black, 6 rows yellow, repeat from * to end. Tape down and stitch outer edges.
Cut bag lining to same size, baste to bag, wrong sides facing, and stitch outer edges together.

Trim bag all round with binding. Fold lower part of bag upwards, matching x to o (see plan). Sew sides invisibly together by hand, stitching through the binding.

GOLD ENVELOPE BAG
Materials:
Wood-pulp board, 31×48cm (12×19in). Cardboard for stiffening, 26×15cm (10×6in). Narrow braid: 75m (82yd) in gold, 1.70m (2yd) brown corded ribbon, 2.5cm (1in) wide. *Lining material:* 30×50cm (12×20in). Strong adhesive tape. Sellotape.

Working instructions:
See photographs for weaving technique. Cut 35 notches in each of the narrow sides of wood-pulp board. Cut following lengths of braid: 35 warp threads 53cm (21in) long, 150 weft threads 34cm (13½in) long.

Cut bag lining to same size as bag; baste together, wrong sides facing, and stitch outer edges together, at the same time inserting cardboard cut to size into lower part of bag to act as stiffening. Bind lower edge of flap with corded ribbon. Fold lower part of bag upwards, matching x to o (see plan). Baste sides together and bind bag all round with corded ribbon.

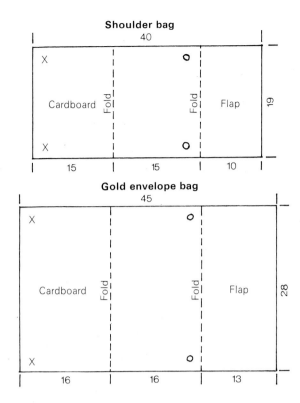

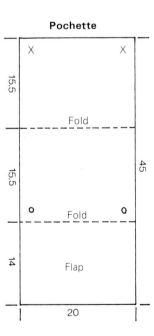

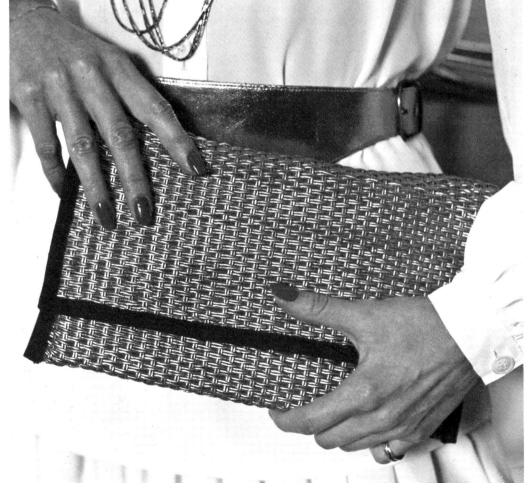

Woven patchwork

This blanket, which consists of squares and oblongs, is made of fabric woven in home-made frames. The individual squares are each 20 × 20cm (8 × 8in) and the oblongs are 10 × 20cm (4 × 8in). Although only four colours are used, an attractive multi-coloured effect results from varying the patterns as you weave. You can make and set up a frame any way you like. Whether you want to weave stripes or checks, a pepper-and-salt effect or a plain rectangle, a square or an oblong, the principle is always the same. First join the woven pieces together with safety pins in strips, so that you can experiment with the arrangement. Then sew the strips together, and join to other strips. Detailed working instructions are given with step-by-step photographs to illustrate the weaving technique.

Weaving in a frame:

All woven fabric must have warp (lengthwise) and weft (across) threads. In this method of weaving, the warp threads are stretched from nails and the weft threads darned through them with a needle. The frame is made of wooden slats and nails. See detail picture, above right.

Materials:

1 A selection of double knitting yarns. *Wooden slats:* 3cm thick (just over 1in). *Nails:* 4 30mm (1in) long nails; nails without heads 12mm (just under $\frac{1}{2}$in) long. Adhesive. Tapestry needles for the weaving. Frame shown here consists of 2 slats 13cm (5in) long and 2 slats 19cm ($7\frac{1}{2}$in) long; the inner area when complete measures 9 × 19cm ($3\frac{1}{2}$ × $7\frac{1}{2}$in).

Working instructions:

Stick slats together with adhesive, then nail at corners, using long nails (bore a hole first to prevent wood splitting). 1cm (just under $\frac{1}{2}$in) in from inner edges of slats, mark places for small nails at intervals of 1cm (just under $\frac{1}{2}$in); at each corner place 3 nails at intervals of 5mm (just under

$\frac{1}{4}$in) apart (the distance between nails can be varied according to the thickness of the yarn).

2 Set up work as follows: to stretch warp threads in frame, make a knot about 25cm (10in) from end of yarn and loop over one of the corner nails. The first warp thread will lie outside the nail, the second directly inside it. Keep stretching warp threads from top to bottom around nails. When end is reached knot thread again and pass it over a corner nail, leaving about 25cm (10in) hanging loose. If stripes or checks are required, set up warp threads in different colours.

3 Now begin weaving with the weft threads, which can also be arranged in different colours. Cut yarn to length that is most comfortable to work with. Pass needle alternately over and under a warp thread; at end of a row pass weft thread around nail and weave back again across warp threads. The last few rows tend to be rather tight because the entire area is now stretched taut. To ease the tension on these rows, divide the rows in working, by weaving from sides to centre. Take care that the run of the threads in the two central rows matches the weave correctly with a neat link-up at the centre.

4 Beginnings and ends of yarn are tied round a nail and later sewn in as the woven pieces are put together. Outer ends of warp threads can be used for joining the pieces (see picture 6).

5 When weaving is finished, lift work over nails and off the frame. The woven fabric will contract to its final size.

6 Sew squares and oblongs together, stitching from loops at edge of one piece to those at edge of another, and darning in loose threads.

1

2

3

4

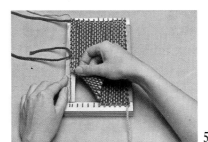

5

6

Appliqué

Farmyard fun

Appliqué is one of the simplest of needlework crafts and anyone who can sew will find it an effective way of creating imaginative and colourful designs from scraps of materials, using a combination of basic sewing and embroidery techniques.

The method involves cutting fabrics into shapes and then stitching them on to a background fabric. You have a choice of fabrics from a wide range – cottons, felts, corded materials and even silks – depending on their use, but always remember that the background fabric should be stronger than the applied fabrics. The embroidered touches described in the working instructions below are intended as ideas for your guidance: you can replace them if desired with other favourite embroidery stitches.

Materials:

Piece of plain foundation material slightly larger than finished picture size (see full-size drawing overleaf); scraps of brightly coloured fabrics or felts and 2 larger pieces for blue sky and flowered grass areas; sewing threads and stranded embroidery cottons; working drawing as described below.

Working instructions:

A full-size drawing of the picture is given overleaf for tracing: trace and transfer as described on page 9. Each motif outline is numbered; the motifs are stitched on the background fabric in this order. The broken lines are given as a guide for applying motifs partly covered by other motifs, which will extend about 6mm ($\frac{1}{4}$in) beyond the broken lines. Trace complete picture and transfer on to foundation. Use drawing again to transfer shapes on to pieces of fabrics or felts for individual motifs and cut these out. Fit in position on background, starting with sky (1), then grass (2). Sew in position as you go along with bold oversewing stitches in sewing cottons.

Some of the motifs have embroidered touches, as shown in the pictures. Suggestions for these are as follows: apples, birds, flowers on grass and in window-boxes in satin stitch; apple and flower stalks and leaves in straight and loop stitches; fence, sunbeams, cottage outlines and cockerel's feathers in stem stitch; ladder and farmer's braces in chain stitch; sunflowers in satin and loop stitches; basket in solid laid threads of several strands, tied with 3 strands. All remaining details are in stem, straight and satin stitches. The apron is a scrap of lace tied with stranded cotton.

Finishing:

Stretch picture over a piece of strong cardboard; turn surplus foundation material to wrong side all round and stick down. Mount picture in colour frame as desired.

Batik magic

If you like to use your imagination, buy plain or patterned fabric by the metre and dye it to your own design by the batik method. It takes time to achieve a delicate pattern such as this one; the more colours you use the longer the work will take. However, the filigree-like effect of the end product is worth the trouble. Batik is not difficult, but it is a craft that requires care, so read through the instructions thoroughly and practise on fabric remnants before you attempt a complete design.

Material dyeing

To illustrate the processes of batik dyeing a neutral-coloured, prettily patterned flower fabric was overprinted with a simple deer motif and dyed in a colour combination

of amethyst, mauve, turquoise and dark green. The graduated colour effect is achieved by overlaying certain areas with different coloured dyes and eliminating other areas as required. Step-by-step photographs illustrate this technique in detail and show the materials required.

Preparing the design:
Draw the design repeat on transparent paper with a felt pen. This drawing is important, since you will be placing it on the fabric again and again. The paper used has a grease-resistant coating, so that when you peel the fabric away from the waxed tracing no little bits of paper will be left adhering to it. In this way the drawing remains intact and can be used over and over again.

Fabric to use:
Those made of natural fibres are most suitable for batik; synthetics do not absorb the batik dyes well, so avoid fabrics with a mixture of man-made fibres. The finer the fabric the better it absorbs hot wax, so if you want really clear outlines use thin silk or cotton.

Equipment for dyeing:
Batik dyes: batik dyes (cold-water dyes are best) can be obtained from stores and do-it-yourself shops. Instructions accompanying them will give directions for their use.
Dye remover: dye-removing powder dissolves in water very quickly.
Batik wax, special batik can with spout, hotplate to melt wax, pan to hold wax: batik wax must be kept very hot on the hotplate all the time the work is in progress. It is applied when almost boiling so that the fabric is well sealed and no dye seeps into the waxed areas later. The parts of the fabric sealed with wax should look transparent; wax that has not permeated the fabric will peel off during the repeated dyeing processes and the design outline will become blurred. The little batik can should be held with its spout perfectly straight, or tilted slightly backwards; if too much wax collects at the small opening, drops that are too thick will fall on the fabric.
Brush: certain areas of the fabric can be wax painted with a brush (see picture 3).
Absorbent paper: make sure it will absorb plenty of wax easily.

1 Some of the material required for batik work.
2 Lay the drawn design on a light-coloured surface, so that you can see the outline easily, then place the fabric over it.
3 Heat the wax almost to boiling point and pour into batik can. Using the spout of the batik can, let the hot wax trace the outline of design on the fabric. The design is now outlined in wax on the fabric. When you have finished tracing the design, lift the fabric carefully off the paper.
4 If several dyes are being used, begin with the lightest: in

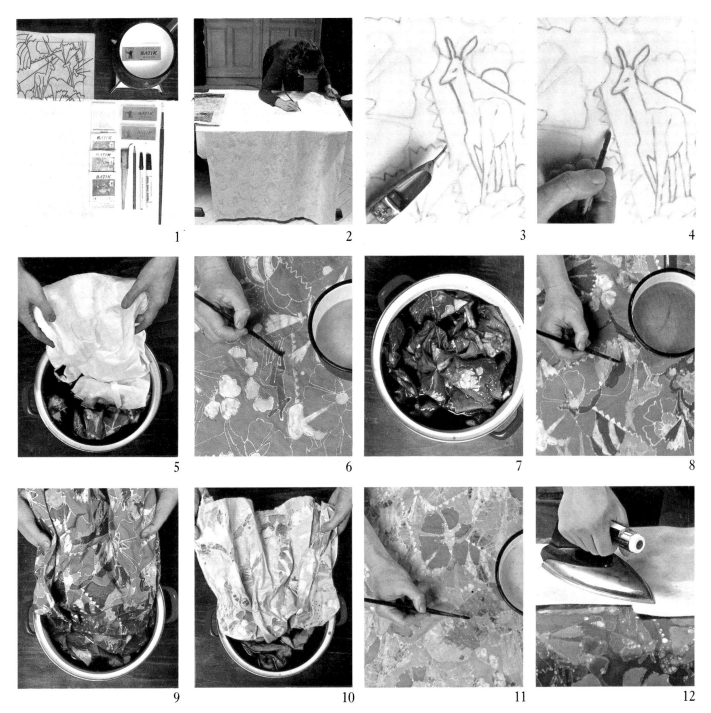

1

2

3

4

5

6

7

8

9

10

11

12

this case, amethyst. Areas which are to remain undyed (in this case, white) are painted over with hot wax; use a brush as in the picture.

5 Now apply the first dye: amethyst. The longer the fabric is left in the dye, the deeper the colour becomes.
After each dyeing, rinse the fabric repeatedly in warm water until the water stays clear. Finally, let the fabric dry.
6 Now those areas of fabric which are to remain amethyst are painted with hot wax. Unwaxed areas will be coloured mauve by overlaying them with the second dye, turquoise.
7 Mix the second dye: turquoise. Dip the fabric in the dye. Those areas not sealed with wax will now be dyed mauve. Rinse and dry the fabric again.
8 Seal the areas which are to remain mauve with wax. As the unsealed parts of the fabric are now all mauve, a dye

remover must be applied to those areas which are to be re-dyed turquoise.
9 Those areas sealed with wax will retain their colour when the fabric is immersed in dye remover, while the areas left unsealed will lose colour.
10 Rinse the fabric well after taking it out of the dye re-mover. Then dip it in the turquoise dye again. Rinse and dry.
11 Now seal those areas which are to remain turquoise. Then dip the fabric in the green dye. The mixture of turquoise and green will turn those areas not sealed with wax dark green.
12 After rinsing and drying, place fabric between layers of absorbent paper. With a hot iron, iron over the paper to remove wax from fabric. Repeat this process until all the wax is removed.

Rugmaking

Warm comfort

The exciting design for this rug is based on the rich, colourful carpets of the orient and, in lovely toning shades of red and brown, looks like a valuable antique. Its clear-cut pattern goes equally well with the uncluttered modern look in furnishing, or with the elegance of an older style. Using cut yarn and the latch hook, you will find this rug enjoyable and soothing to work.

The beauty of the design shows best on a large rug. Nevertheless, the basic simplicity of the individual shapes is such that the design could be adapted to smaller sizes by careful planning.

When completed, the rug measures approximately 1.40m (56in) square.

Materials:
Rug wool in cut packs as follows: 53 packs dark brown; 23 packs rust; 18 packs old rose; 26 packs beige; 33 packs natural white. Rug canvas with approximately 16 threads to 7cm (3in): 170 × 140cm (66 × 54in) wide. Latch hook.

Working instructions:
As wool is cut, this rug is easy to work, and, using the latch hook, you will find the work goes along very quickly. See page 9 for working knot and hints on finishing.

The colour chart shows a quarter section of rug. Begin at bottom left corner about 10cm (4in) up from edge of canvas and follow each row on chart by working up to centre stitch, then back to complete row. The rug is best worked continuously from bottom to top. When bottom half of design is completed, work top half to match. Finally turn in surplus canvas at top and bottom of rug and face with carpet binding.

Dark brown
53 packs

Rust
23 packs

Old rose
18 packs

Beige
26 packs

Natural white
33 packs

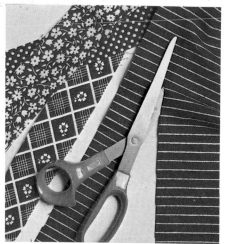

Playroom magic

This is a quick-and-easy way of making a rug for a children's room. By working in cross stitch with remnants of fabric, each square is completed in next to no time to build up into a gay patchwork effect.

The original rug was worked in an assortment of red cottons, but of course it would look just as attractive in other colours. Look on the remnant counters of your local stores for suitable materials, or use whatever comes to hand at home.

The rug is worked in straight rows of cross stitch which will form squares. The squares are arranged so that the grain of the lines of embroidery runs alternately lengthwise and crosswise. 1 square is approximately 10×10cm (4×4in) large. Strips of fabric are used as embroidery thread, and a safety pin is the embroidery needle. The rug is embroidered on squared canvas.

Materials:

Original rug is about 90×125cm (36×49in), but this will depend on your choice of canvas and remnants. Each square takes about 25cm (10in) of fabric 80cm (32in) wide. Strips of different remnants of fabric: approximately 20m (22yd) in all. For border squares: about 10m (11yd) plain coloured cotton. For the backing: squared rug canvas, 1m (just over 3ft) wide and about 1.40m (2½yd) long. A large safety pin. Sharp scissors for cutting.

Working instructions:

The detailed pictures show you how to work the rug. Cut fabric into strips 70cm (27½in) long and about 3.5cm (just under 1½in) wide. It is not essential to cut them exactly to the nearest millimetre!

Place strips right side down, turn both edges under and press lightly. This makes it easier to work the cross stitch with them. With pressed edges turned under so that fabric is double, put a safety pin through end of strip. Now stitch through canvas, bringing 'needle' through from back of work. Pass needle diagonally from bottom left to top right over canvas, then pass through work from right side. Bring up again in the third square down, stitch through work from right side again, and continue in this way.

When 7 stitches have been worked one way across a row, work back to form cross stitch. As you work, be careful to keep the raw edges of the fabric tucked under.

3×3 squares in canvas=1 cross, 7 crosses=1 row, and 7 rows=1 square. The rug consists of 117 squares.

Once all the squares of rug have been worked on the backing canvas, canvas edges are trimmed to about 5cm (2in) all round, turned under and stitched to back of rug (use large stitches). Loose ends of 'threads' at beginning and end of rows can simply be left loose at back of work, or trimmed to about 4cm (1½in).

If preferred, the rug can be given an additional backing of some coarse material such as hessian. If the rug is to lie on a slippery floor, it is advisable to place a piece of rubber matting underneath to stop it sliding about.

A round of colour

Why not a round rug for a change? There is something cosy and attractive about round rugs, and this modern design in rich deep colours is strikingly unusual. The background of the rug is a warm brown, which sets off the brighter shades of rusty reds and greens. Abstract motifs make it suitable for any setting.

The rug measures about 145cm (57in) in diameter. It is worked on rug canvas, using the simple hooking method.

Materials:

Rug canvas with approximately 10 threads to 7cm (3in): 150cm (60in) square. Rug wool in cut packs (320 strands to a pack). Amounts and colours are shown on the colour key.

You will also need 200g sks of uncut wool for the edging. Latch hook for rugmaking. See page 9 for working knot and hints on finishing.

The colour chart shows half the rug in detail. Follow the same pattern all round. Begin with the first short row 7cm (3in) from edge of canvas and work the first half of rug, then work second half to match. The colour key shows the shade of wool to be used and the corresponding colour on the pattern chart.

When you have finished hooking the rug, cut the canvas to within about 5cm (2in) of the work all round and turn under, leaving an edge about 1–2cm ($\frac{1}{2}$–$\frac{3}{4}$in) wide. Using rug wool and a crochet hook No 5mm (UK No 6), work single crochet all round edge, or cover edge with binding stitch. Finally sew carpet binding to back of rug.

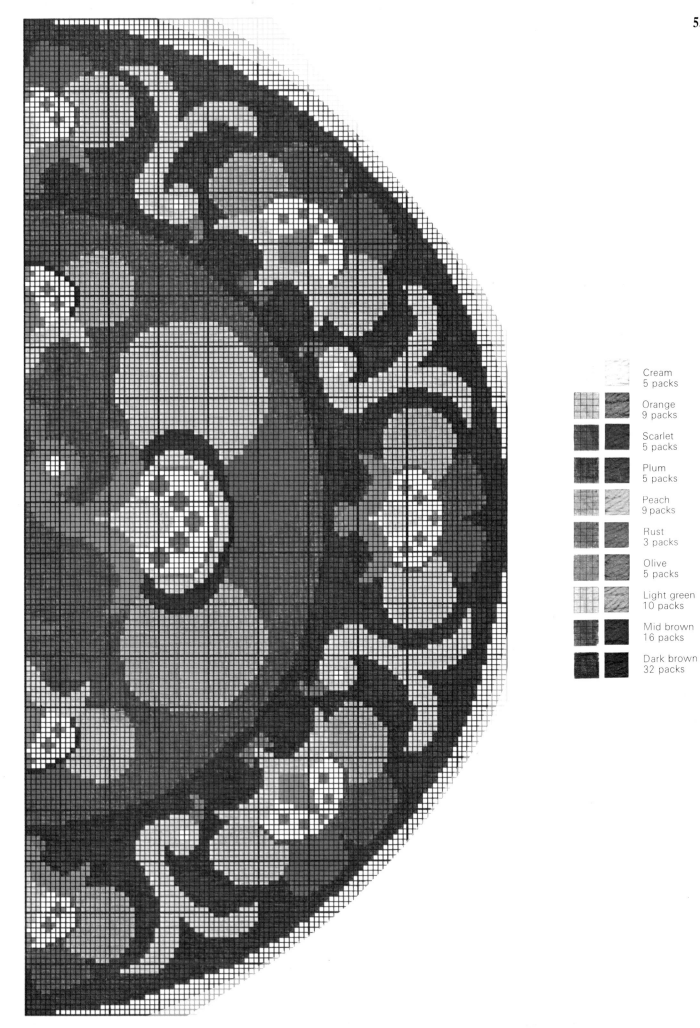

Cream
5 packs

Orange
9 packs

Scarlet
5 packs

Plum
5 packs

Peach
9 packs

Rust
3 packs

Olive
5 packs

Light green
10 packs

Mid brown
16 packs

Dark brown
32 packs

Step by step

You can decide on the size of your own rug, which is made of separate 'carpet tiles' sewn together. Each tile measures 11×11cm ($4\frac{1}{4} \times 4\frac{1}{4}$in), a handy size which will make your work easier. Squares are worked in crochet, using slip stitch on canvas, and instructions are given for six different designs for you to mix and match or choose one only for an overall effect. Original rug squares were worked in thick yarn on a large-mesh canvas, but the size of the square can be varied according to materials used.

Size
Each side of a tile = 11cm ($4\frac{1}{4}$in).

Materials
Rug yarn in black, beige, red-brown, ochre and tobacco; 25g in assorted colours for each tile. 1 crochet hook No 6.00mm (UK size 4). Backing material: large-mesh rug canvas.

Design:
Tiles are worked in slip stitch crocheted through canvas.

Working instructions:
Cut a square of canvas measuring 19 mesh squares each way for every tile. Turn in 2 mesh squares all round the edge; during work crochet 2 mesh squares together at edges. When sewing up do not pull beginning and end threads tight; end thread can be taken over to adjoining tile and then sewn in.

Pattern 1: Starting in 4th mesh square from bottom and left-hand edges, work 3 rows each in ochre, black and tobacco, each row filling 9 mesh squares. Round this central square work 1 round in beige, 2 rounds in red-brown.

Pattern 2: Work 3 rows each in black, ochre, red-brown, beige and tobacco across entire width of tile.

Pattern 3: Work 9 small squares in different colours. Bring

up yarn in 3rd mesh square from bottom and side edges, work 1 sl st into mesh square to the left, then work into square vertically above, continue working thus in a spiral, filling 5 mesh squares each way. Start each new square of pattern 3 mesh squares away from previous pattern square.

Pattern 4: Starting at left-hand bottom corner, bring up yarn and make a loop, insert hook into mesh square above, work 1 sl st, work following sl sts 1 to the left, 1 vertically down = 1 row. Continue working back and forth in the same way round this first corner; work 5 rows beige, 2 rows each in red-brown, ochre, tobacco and black.

Pattern 5: Starting in central mesh square, bring up yarn and make a loop, then work 1 sl st to the left, 1 sl st diagonally up into square above centre, 1 sl st into square right of centre, then into square below centre and into square to

left of centre. Continue working thus in a diamond shape until you reach the outer edges. When turning the round, always work 1 sl st into square to the left of last round; at end of round work into same square. Work 1 triangle each in red-brown, ochre, tobacco and black to fill corners: work first along side of diamond shape, then along outer edge and thus inward, working in a spiral.

Pattern 6: Starting in the middle, work as described in Pattern 3, 1 pattern square over 3 mesh squares each way. Then work 2 rounds in tobacco, 1 round each in black and red-brown, 2 rounds in ochre.

Making up:
Stitch tiles together on wrong side with an oversewing stitch, using a few strands of the rug yarn, or twine.

Beadwork

Jewel-bright trims

These beadwork accessories are unusual and fashionable. They are made of tiny embroidery beads threaded in strings and stuck in place on a foundation article to form stripes, flowers and ornamental motifs. The pendants and purse are made of leather, and the bangles of wood.

BANGLES
Materials:
Wooden bangles, strong two-component adhesive, strong sewing thread. *Top bangle:* 10g each of embroidery beads in white and green, 20g in blue. *Middle bangle:* 10g each in pink, brown, yellow, orange and red. *Bottom bangle:* 10g each in green, light blue, dark brown and turquoise.

Working instructions:
The technique is as follows: beads are threaded on sewing thread in the desired colour combinations. The wooden bangle is painted with adhesive and the string of beads wound round it.

String beads on thread cut to a normal length. Thread beads on a smooth surface, so that they can be picked up easily. String about 40 beads of colour desired and stick to part of bangle to which adhesive has been applied (apply adhesive only to the area where the beads are about to be glued in position). Leave for a short while to allow beads to stick firmly in place. Then string more beads and glue in position again. Continue in this way until a section of bangle

about 2cm ($\frac{3}{4}$in) wide has been covered. Then glue a little thread without beads in place to adjust the beadwork to the inside curve of bangle. Continue as before. The next row of beads will cover the length of bare thread. Repeat this process every 2cm ($\frac{3}{4}$in). When thread comes to an end begin with a new length, knotting ends of the 2 threads together, but make sure that beads can be threaded over the knot.

PENDANTS
Materials:
Remnants of leather, leather needle, strong sewing thread, embroidery beads as follows: *Left-hand pendant:* 10g each in green, turquoise and dark brown. *Right-hand pendant:* 10g each in white, red and blue.

Working instructions:
Cut 2 pieces of leather 3cm (1in) wide and 7cm (2$\frac{3}{4}$in) long for back and front of bag. Cut 1 strip 1.5cm (just over $\frac{1}{2}$in) wide and 19cm (7$\frac{1}{2}$in) long for the strip to fit down sides and base of bag. For strap, cut 1 strip 5mm (just under $\frac{1}{4}$in) wide and 75cm (29$\frac{1}{2}$in) long; sew this inside top edges of side strip. With wrong sides facing, stitch front, back and side strips of bag together, close to edge, leaving edges raw. Thread beads separately for each side and stitch to bag, passing needle through existing stitching lines at seams.

BELT PURSE
Materials:
Remnant of leather, leather needle, strong adhesive, strong sewing thread, embroidery beads: 50g in blue, 10g each in black, green, red and yellow.

Working instructions:

Make a paper pattern for purse from the plan below. The flower motif is shown full size (left): trace it on tissue paper for transferring to flap of purse, using pencil and carbon paper. Cut purse from leather in one piece, with no seam allowance. For fastening, cut 2 strips each 5mm (just under ¼in) wide and about 18cm (7in) long; stitch to bag at right angles as shown in plan. Make up bag as shown in plan and bind in edges to depth of 5mm. Reinforce flap of bag with a stout piece of leather. Then trace flower motif on outside of flap. String beads (for colour scheme see photograph; for method see also instructions for bracelets). Here the strings of beads are glued on in a circular pattern; wind the work from the inside outwards. Use plenty of adhesive; ease beads into place at curved edges of design with a needle.

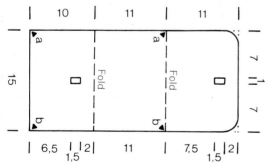

Soft toys

Pet's corner

Soft but firm, and in such pretty colours, these animals are just the thing for children to cuddle and play with. They are made of needlecord, fur fabric, cotton, hessian and felt, but the smaller animals could easily be made from remnants you already have. For filling, kapok and pre-cut foam chips have been used. You can adjust the amount of filling according to how soft or firm you want the finished toy to be.

Paper patterns
Make up paper patterns from the graph-paper plans by copying the appropriate shapes and scaling up to correct size (for instructions on scaling up see page 9). Then cut out paper shapes to make the actual size pattern for each animal.

PIGLET
Materials:
Pink needlecord: 30cm (12in) of fabric 150cm (60in) wide; scrap of blue felt for eyes; 30cm (12in) wire for tail; filling.

Cutting out:
See instructions for scaling up pattern layout on page 9. Body: cut 2. Lower body and back of body: cut 1 each with fabric double, laying pattern piece against fold. Ear and sole of foot: cut 4. Snout: cut 1. Cut strip 30cm (12in) long and 3cm (1in) wide for tail, cut circles for eyes. Allow 6mm (just under ¼in) seam allowance for all parts.

Making up:
Stitch back of body to lower body. Stitch this part to both body pieces. Leave open joins for snout and soles of feet. Sew together ears, leaving join with head open, and turn right side out.
Now close upper seam of body, leaving opening for the filling, and fitting ears in place. Stitch on snout and soles of feet. Turn piglet's body right side out and stuff it. Sew up opening in seam by hand. Stitch together and turn right side out the strip for tail, inserting wire into it. Sew tail to top point of back of body. Glue on eyes.

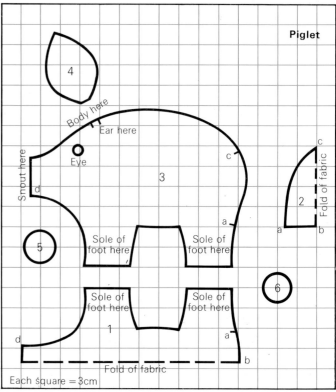

Each square = 3cm

1 Lower body
2 Back of body
3 Body
4 Ear
5 Snout
6 Sole of foot

Enlarge all plans for toys on this and the following pages by scaling up as described on page 9. Measurements are in centimetres.

PIG
Materials:
Pink needlecord: 80cm (32in) of fabric 150cm (60in) wide; scrap of blue felt for eyes; 40cm (16in) wire for tail; filling.

Cutting out:
See instructions for piglet. You will also need a strip of fabric 40cm (16in) long and 3cm (1in) wide for tail, plus seam allowance.

Making up:
As for piglet.

LION
Materials:
Yellow needlecord: 95cm (38in) of fabric 150cm (60in) wide.

Brown needlecord: 10cm (4in) of fabric 150cm (60in) wide; 150g brown wool; string for whiskers; filling.

Cutting out:
Cut from yellow needlecord: 2 body pieces, 1 each of lower body and back of body from double fabric, laying pattern pieces against fold. Head: cut 2; middle part of head, cut 2 from double fabric, laying piece against fold. Tail: cut 2. Ear and sole of foot: cut 4 each in brown fabric. 6mm (just under $\frac{1}{4}$in) seam allowance. Eyes: cut 2 circles of brown fabric.

1 Lower body
2 Back of body
3 Body
4 Ear
5 Snout
6 Sole of foot

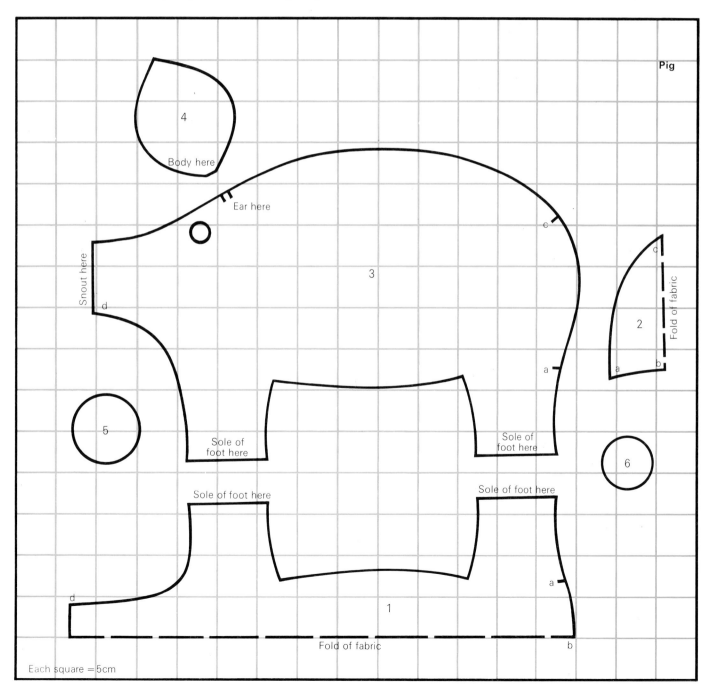

Each square = 5cm

Making up:

Close upper seam of body (a–b) leaving an opening for filling. Stitch back of body to lower part of body. Now stitch this part to both body parts. Leave open the joins for soles of feet. Finally close short cross-seam a–f. Stitch on soles of feet. Turn body right side out.

Work the head: stitch together ears and turn right side out, leaving join with head open. Stitch together middle part of head as far as the curve, then stitch to head, leaving an opening for filling, and fitting the ears into front seam. Turn head right side out.

Now fill body and head. Stitch up openings by hand. Stitch tail, turn right side out, and stuff.

Knot several strands of wool to end of tail. Embroider three claws with wool on each foot. Embroider face, glue on eyes, and thread string through face for whiskers. Cut remaining wool into strands and knot to middle part of head to make the mane.

BEAR

Materials:

Black fur fabric: 30cm (12in) of fabric 140cm (54in) wide; white fur fabric: 15cm (6in) of fabric 140cm (54in) wide; 2 glass eyes; 1 button for nose; scrap of white felt for insides of ears; filling.

Cutting out:

From black fur fabric, cut 2 body pieces. Head and lower body: cut 2 each; middle part of head, cut 1 from white fur fabric, double, laying pattern piece against fold. Ears: cut 2 each from black fur fabric and white felt. 6mm (just under $\frac{1}{4}$in) seam allowance for all parts. Eyes: cut 2 circles of black fur fabric with no seam allowance.

Making up:

First stitch lower part of body together as far as the curve (a–b). Stitch this part to both parts of the body. Close upper seam of body.

Now stitch middle part of head to both head pieces. Stitch head to body, leaving an opening for filling. Turn bear right

1 Body   2 Lower body   3 Back of body   4 Sole of foot
5 Head   6 Middle part of head   7 Ear   8 Tail

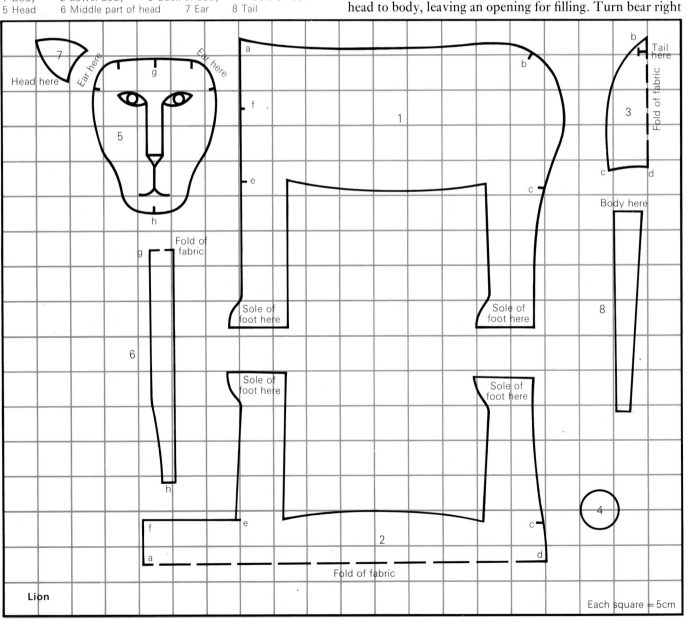

Lion

Each square = 5cm

side out and stuff. Stitch opening together by hand. Stitch together ears, turn right side out, and sew in place as indicated by markings.

Sew on felt circles and glass eyes. Sew on button for nose.

PENGUIN (illustrated overleaf)
Materials:
Black stretch cotton towelling: 20cm (8in) of fabric 140cm (54in) wide; white stretch cotton towelling: 15cm (6in) of

fabric 140cm (54in) wide; scraps of red and flowered cotton; 2 buttons for eyes; filling.

Cutting out:
From black fabric: cut 2 each of body and wing; cut 2 more wings from flowered fabric. From white fabric: cut 1 breast piece. From red fabric: beak, cut 2, foot, cut 4. 6mm (just under $\frac{1}{4}$in) seam allowance for all parts.

Making up:
Use small, even, zig-zag stitching to sew stretch towelling. Stitch beak to both parts of body. Stitch wings together up to join with body and stuff lightly. Stitch breast piece to both parts of body, fitting in wings.

Close up rest of seam from breast to tail, leaving an opening. Turn body right side out, and fill. Stitch feet together, turn right side out and sew to body as indicated. Sew on buttons for eyes.

1 Body	1 Body
2 Lower body	2 Beak
3 Head	3 Breast
4 Middle part of head	4 Wing
5 Ear	5 Foot

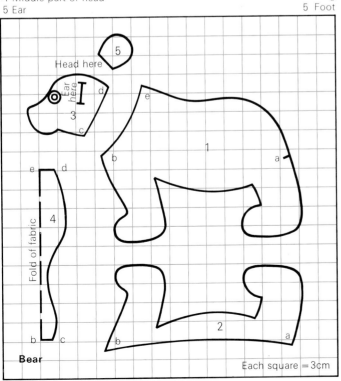
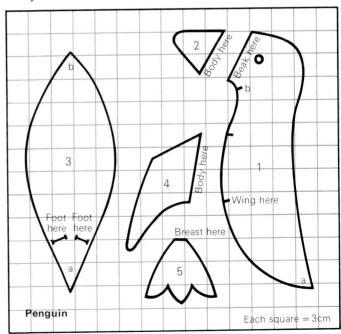

HARE
Materials:
Brown fur fabric: 25cm (10in) of fabric 140cm (54in) wide; white fur fabric: 20cm (8in) of fabric 140cm (54in) wide; 2 glass eyes; scrap of pink embroidery thread for nose; filling.

Cutting out:
From brown fur fabric: cut 2 pieces of body, 1 of middle of head. From white fur fabric: cut 2 pieces each of head and lower body. Ears: cut 2 each in brown and white fur fabric. 6mm (just under $\frac{1}{4}$in) seam allowance for all parts.

Making up:
Stitch head pieces and tail to appropriate parts of body. Stitch middle part of head to head. Stitch lower part of body together along straight edge, leaving an opening for filling; then stitch this part to both body pieces.
Now close upper seam of body from head to tail. Turn hare right side out. Stitch together ears and turn right side out. Fill the hare. Stitch opening in seam by hand.
Fold ears lengthwise and stitch into place as indicated by pattern markings. Sew on eyes. Embroider nose at tip of middle part of head.

ELEPHANT
Materials:
Grey needlecord: 75cm (30in) of fabric 150cm (60in) wide; mauve needlecord: 20cm (8in) of fabric 150cm (60in) wide; scrap of white felt for tusks; scraps of navy blue and white felt for eyes; remnant of grey wool for tail; filling.
Covering: 1 piece of felt 51 × 19cm (20 × 7$\frac{1}{2}$in) in red, 1 piece the same size in white; scraps of green, navy blue, grey and white felt for the pattern.

Cutting out:
From grey needlecord: cut 2 each of body and tail; with fabric double, cut 1 each of lower body and back of body, breast, and middle part of head, laying pattern pieces along fold. From mauve needlecord: cut 4 soles of feet, 1 trunk piece. Ears: cut 2 each in grey and mauve. 6mm (just under $\frac{1}{4}$in) seam allowance. Cut 4 tusk pieces and 2 ovals for eyes from white felt. Cut 2 circles for eyes from navy-blue felt. For the pattern on the covering: cut 4 blue flowers, 2 circles each in grey and white, 2 pairs of stems and leaves in green.

Making up:
First stitch on eyes. Then stitch breast and back part of body to lower body. Stitch this part to both body pieces. Close top seam of trunk. Stitch middle part of head to head. Close upper seam of body, leaving an opening for filling. Stitch

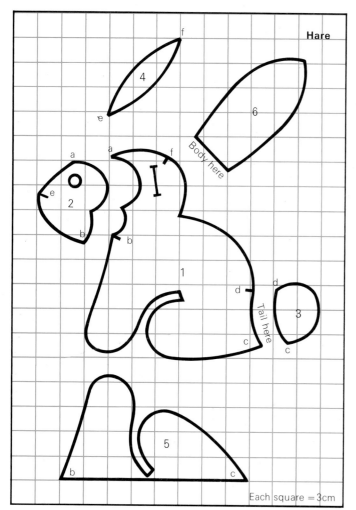

Each square = 3cm

Hare

1 Body
2 Head
3 Tail
4 Middle part of body
5 Lower body
6 Ear

end of trunk to trunk. Stitch soles of feet in place. Turn elephant right side out and fill. Stitch opening by hand. Stitch ears together and sew in to place, turning top of ear 1.5cm ($\frac{1}{2}$in) outwards. Stitch tail together, fill, and sew into place. Knot several strands of wool at end of tail. Stitch tusks together, without turning edges in, fill and sew into place. *Covering:* Stitch 2 pieces of felt together, without turning edges in (red on top, white underneath). Stitch a rectangle 31 × 19cm (12 × 7$\frac{1}{2}$in) in middle; cut fringes at sides. Stitch flower patterns into place.

1 Lower body
2 Breast
3 Back part of body
4 Body
5 Middle part of head
6 End of trunk
7 Sole of foot
8 Ear
9 Tail
10 Tusk
11 Pattern for covering

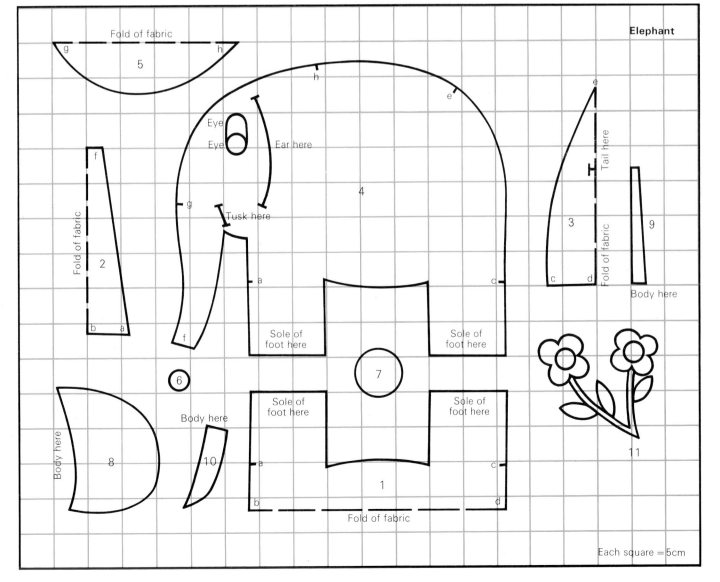

64

HIPPOPOTAMUS

Materials:

Red hessian: 80cm (32in) of fabric 130cm (52in) wide; beige hessian: 30cm (12in) of fabric 130cm (52in) wide; 75cm (30in) covered wire for face; scrap of blue felt for eyes; scrap of green hessian for pattern on covering.

Cutting out:

From red hessian: cut 2 body pieces; with fabric double, cut 1 each of upper and lower body laying pattern piece along fold. Also from red: cut 2 head pieces with the fabric double, cut 1 each of middle part of head and of tail, laying pattern piece along fold. From beige hessian: cut 4 soles of feet; cut 2 each of ears in red and beige. 1cm (just under ½in) seam allowance on all parts. Eyes: cut 2 ovals of beige hessian and 2 circles of felt.

For the covering: cut 1 piece from beige hessian with fabric double, laying pattern piece along fold, with about 1cm (just under ½in) seam allowance. Cut 6 triangles (4 red, 2 green), without seam allowance, for the pattern.

Making up:

Stitch upper and lower body pieces together along short cross-seams. Stitch this part to both body pieces, leaving an opening for filling. Stitch soles of feet in place.

Now work the head: stitch together ears, as far as join with head, and turn to right side. Close seam of middle part of head as far as the curve. Then stitch to both parts of head, leaving an opening for filling, and fitting ears in place as indicated by pattern markings. Turn body and head right side out and fill. Stitch openings by hand.

Stitch together tail, turn right side out, and sew in place. Glue eyes to head and the covered wire to face as shown in the plan. Now sew head to body.

Trim round covering, stitch down seam allowance. Trim triangles and stitch to covering.

1 Shell piece
2 Lower body
3 Feet
4 Head

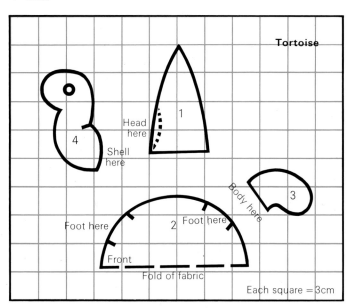

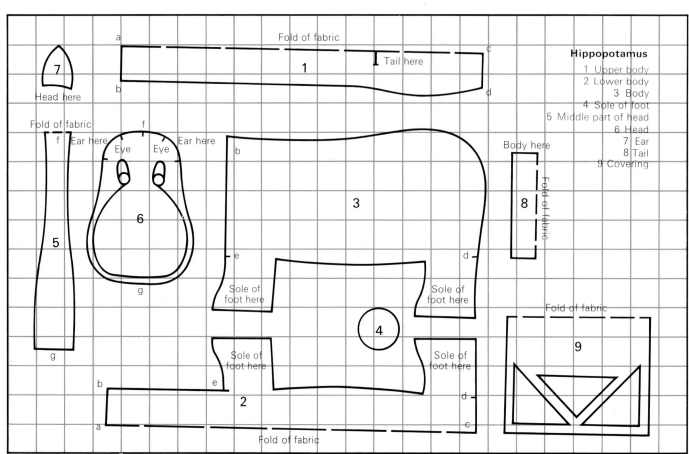

cotton fabric double: cut 1 lower body, laying pattern piece along fold. 6mm (just under $\frac{1}{4}$in) seam allowance for all parts.

TORTOISE

Materials:

Plain stretch cotton towelling: 10cm (4in) of fabric 140cm (54in) wide; striped stretch cotton towelling: 15cm (6in) of fabric 140cm (54in) wide; scrap of plain cotton; 2 glass eyes; filling.

Cutting out:

From striped towelling fabric: cut 8 shell pieces. From plain towelling fabric: cut 2 head pieces and 8 feet. With plain

Making up:

Sew stretch cotton towelling with small, even, zig-zag stitches. Stitch together shell pieces along long sides, leaving a space to fit head between two shell pieces. Stitch together head pieces and feet as far as the joins with body and shell, turn right side out. Fill. Stitch shell to the lower body, leaving an opening for filling, and turn right side out.

The join with head is at the front; fit feet in place as indicated by pattern markings. Sew head in place. Fill tortoise's body, stitch opening by hand. Sew on eyes.

Mick the monk

This lovable giant monkey is sure to be popular. He makes a delightful toy for children, or a snug and comfortable floor cushion for a lazy half-hour.

Materials:

2.30m (2½yd) of 140cm (54in) wide dark fur fabric; 40cm (16in) of 140cm (54in) wide light fur fabric; metal buttons and scrap of felt for eyes; embroidery thread for mouth and nostrils; strong sewing cotton; 160cm (1¾yd) cord. For the filling: 2 foam-filled cushion pads, 35 × 40 × 4cm (14 × 16 × 1½in) for the body; for the other parts, 3 packets of foam chips, 1500g (about 3lb).

Cutting out:

See instructions for scaling up pattern layout on page 9.
Cut from a single layer of dark fur fabric: body with legs, cut 2 as a complete oblong; arm, cut 4; front of head, cut 2. With dark fur fabric folded, cut back of head 1, laying pattern piece along fold. With light fur fabric, single: face, cut 2; hands, feet and ears, cut 4 each.
Seam allowance: none on front head pieces where they join face. Allow 1cm (½in) for hands, feet and ears and 2cm (¾in) for rest.

Making up:

First stitch side seams of body from join with arms downwards, and outer seams of legs very firmly, right sides facing. Between legs, make two firm lines of stitching 4cm (1½in) apart; cut away material between these seams and trim at corners. Stitch short seams 5cm (2in) long at bottoms of legs where they will join feet (see plan).
Close shoulder seams. Now turn fabric to right side. Stitch through both layers of fabric at top of legs. Stuff legs loosely with foam chips from tops of legs to knees. Stitch through both legs at knee. Then stuff rest of legs.
Stitch together feet up to join with leg, and turn right side out. Stitch along stitching lines for toes, then hand-stitch feet to legs. Now work arms: stitch seams, leaving two joins for body and hand open, and turn fabric right side out.
Stitch together hands, turn right side out. Stitch along stitching lines for fingers, then hand-stitch to arms. Now fill lower part of arms loosely with foam chips. Stitch through arms at elbows. Fill upper part of arms. Hand-stitch arms to body. Fill lower part of body with one of the foam-cushion pads. Hand-stitch through middle of body. Fill upper part of body with other cushion pad.
Now work head: join two front head pieces to two halves of face, using a zig-zag stitch. Then close centre seam down front of head and face. Stitch together front and back of head, turn to right side, leaving joins with body and ear open.
Stitch together ears, turn to right side of fabric, stitch a line 1cm (½in) just inside edges of the ears. Hand-stitch ears to head. Cover buttons with felt and sew on to face for eyes. Work nostrils with French knots and mouth in stem-stitch. Sew front of the head to body by hand, fill with foam chips, then sew back of head to body.
Sew 40cm (16in) lengths of cord to insides of arms at wrists, and tops of legs.

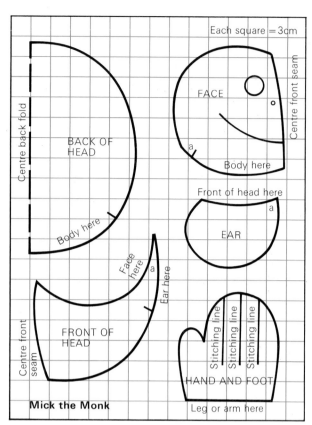

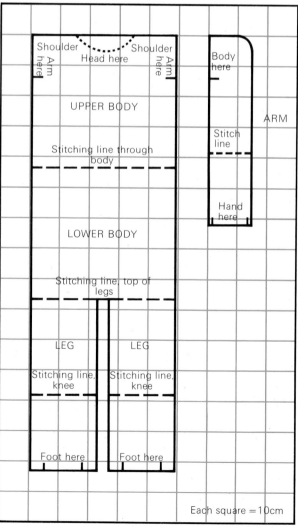

Puppets' parade

Great fun for the children! These animals
will jump
performance, or act plays with them. You can use
anything your collection of remnants has to offer to
make these amusing puppets: remnants of brightly
coloured fabric, scraps of leather and felt, wool,
string, coloured embroidery threads and all sorts of
different wooden beads.

To work each puppet, you need two small pieces of wood,
to which nylon cords are attached with beads. All you have
to do is fasten the animals to the cords – and teach them to
dance! However, you can omit the cords to keep the toys as
lovable pets – they are so soft and cuddly and will give your
children hours of pleasure.

Paper patterns:
Make up paper patterns from the graph patterns by copying
the appropriate shapes and scaling up to correct size (for
instructions on scaling up see page 9). Then cut out paper
shapes to make the actual size pattern for each animal puppet.

Materials for all the puppets:
Remnants of fabric, thin nylon cord, wooden slats 9mm
($\frac{1}{3}$in) thick, wooden beads, wire, 1 small hook, kapok or foam
for filling.

Extra material for individual puppets:
Dachshund: Brown leather for the face, insides of the ears
and tail. 2 wooden beads for eyes.
Cat: 2 wooden beads for eyes. Thin string for whiskers.

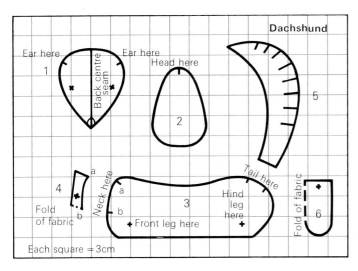

Dachshund

1 Head
2 Ear
3 Body
4 Neck
5 Tail
6 Leg

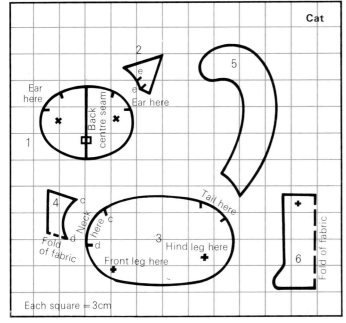

1 Head
2 Ear
3 Body
4 Neck
5 Tail
6 Leg

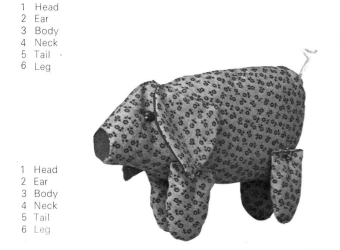

Cat

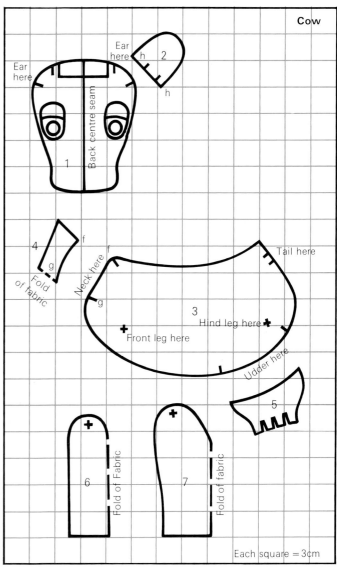

Cow

1 Head
2 Ear
3 Body
4 Neck
5 Udder
6 Front leg
7 Hind leg

1 Body
2 Ear
3 Tail
4 Leg

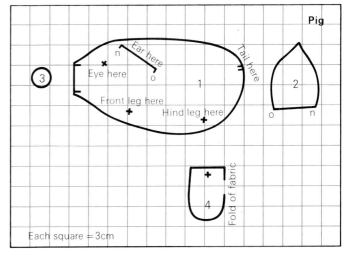

Pig

Cow: Cotton yarn for tail and the part above the eyes. Felt or leather for the eyes, horns and eyelashes.
Donkey: Wool for the mane and tail. 2 large wooden beads for eyes. Brown leather for the face.
Sheep: 2 wooden beads for the eyes.
Pig: 2 wooden beads for eyes, a pipe cleaner for the tail.

Cutting out:

Seam allowance of 5 to 7mm (about $\frac{1}{4}$in), for all parts except: *dachshund*, no seam allowance for tail except where it joins body; *cow*, no seam allowance for eyes.

All animals: Cut legs double along fold of fabric. Cut 2 body pieces. Cut front of head in one piece, back of head with centre seam for stuffing, as shown in the plan. Cut throat double along fold of fabric.

Sewing up:

Heads (all animals except the pig): Stitch ears together and turn right side out. Close up neck seam opposite the fold; when closing seam in back of head, fit in the straight edge of neck.

Stitch together back and front pieces of head, leaving open the space between ears; fit in ears (stitch firmly along the seam allowance first); turn head right side out and fill it. Close opening in seam by hand.

Bodies (all animals except the pig): Make tails. Dachshund: Glue two pieces of leather together, making a number of cuts along rounded edge. Cat: Stitch tail together, leaving join with body open, and turn to right side. Cow: Crochet or plait a tail 20cm (8in) long. Donkey: The tail is made of 20 strands of wool 20cm (8in) long, knotted together at one end. Sheep: Stitch tail together, leaving open the join with body, and turn to right side.

Pig: Bend a pipe cleaner into a curly shape. Stitch pig's ears together, leaving straight side open, and turn to right side; turn in seam allowance along straight side and stitch ears to pig along line marked o–n.

All animals: Stitch bodies together, leaving open the joins with neck, and turn fabric to right side. (Pig: stitch body together leaving snout open.) Fix tails in place. Fill bodies.

All animals except pig: Turn in seam allowances at join with neck; stitch neck in place.

Pig: Sew on snout by hand.

Legs (all animals): Sew together and turn to right side, leaving straight, narrow end open for filling; after filling, turn in seam allowances here and stitch across tops of legs. Fasten legs to bodies with wire at points marked; holes may be punched first if you have a punching tool. Bend ends of wire into a curved shape.

Assembling puppets (all animals except pig):

Fasten nylon cords behind both ears, each cord being 50cm (20in) long. Fasten a cord about 55cm (22in) long at end of body. Cut a wooden slat 22cm ($8\frac{1}{2}$in) long and another 10cm (4in) long; make a hole about 6mm ($\frac{1}{4}$in) from end. Pull the cords from animals' heads through holes on smaller slat and secure with wooden beads. Fasten smaller slat to one end of longer one with wire so that it can move easily. Pull cord from the body through hole at other end and secure with a bead.

Pig: For the pig you need only 2 cords about 50cm (20in) long, one fastened at the head and the other at the end of body. You also need a slat 20cm (8in) long.

Before finally securing the cords, make sure the puppet is well balanced. Screw the hook by which to hang up the puppet into middle of longer slat.

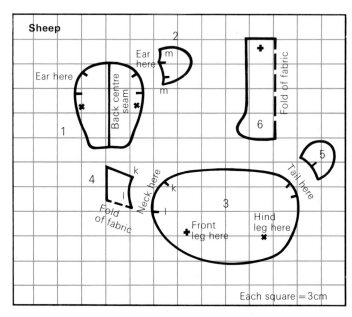

1 Head
2 Ear
3 Body
4 Neck
5 Tail
6 Leg

1 Head
2 Ear
3 Body
4 Neck
5 Front leg
6 Hind leg

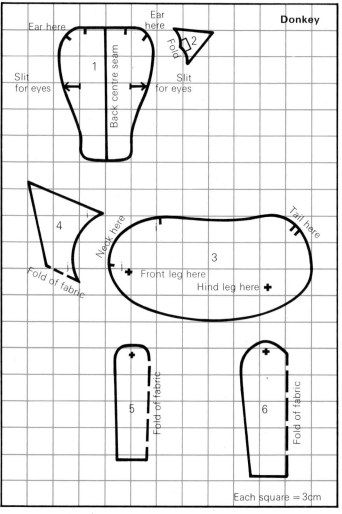

This dachshund can wag his tail and wiggle his ears. You only have to pull the cords.

The cat has a long tail. Her eyes are wooden beads, her whiskers are made of string.

The lamb has a soft fleece of teddy-bear fabric, head and legs of flowered material, and gentle round eyes.

This donkey has a woollen mane, and his face is made of soft leather.

See the cow flutter her long felt eyelashes! She is made of flowered fabric.

Fashion and family knitting

Family gathering

Outdoor jumpers for the whole family: father, mother and child all in jumpers knitted to the same pattern in different shades of blue with striped revers and borders. The collar is knitted separately in striped rib and sewn in place. All three jumpers are child's play to knit. Wear them as overtops with finer polosweaters underneath.

ALL GARMENTS
Materials:
4 ply knitting yarn, used double. 1 pair each knitting needles Nos 4½mm and 5mm (UK sizes 7 and 6).

Stripe sequence:
Casting on row + 1 wrong-side row blue, *2 rows white, 2 rows blue, rep from *.

Tension:
17 sts and 23 rows = 10cm (4in).

WOMAN'S JUMPER
Sizes:
To fit bust 86–91cm and 97–102cm (34–36in and 38–40in). Figures in square brackets [ ] refer to second size.

Materials:
650 [700]g yarn in mid blue, 100 [100]g in white.

Working instructions:
Back: With No 4½mm needles cast on 82 [88] sts in blue and work 13 rows in K1, P1 rib, foll stripe sequence.
Continue working in st st in blue, on No 5mm needles, until work measures 45cm (17½in). Shape armholes by casting off 7 sts at beg of next 2 rows = 68 [74] sts.
Continue working straight, until work measures 65 [67]cm, 25½ [26¼]in.
Shape shoulders by casting off 21 [24] sts at beg of next 2 rows. On rem 26 sts (right side of work), P 1 row, then work 3cm (1in) in st st for back neckband. Cast off.
Front: Work as for back until work measures 45 [47]cm, 17¾ [18½]in.
Shape neck: *next row:* work 21 [24] sts, cast off 26, work to end. Continue on each group of sts until work measures 65 [67]cm, 25½ [26¼]in. Cast off.
Sleeves: With No 4½mm needles, cast on 46 [52] sts in blue and work 13 rows K1, P1 rib, foll stripe sequence.
Continue working in st st in blue on No 5mm needles, inc 1 st at each end of every 8th row 10 times = 66 [72] sts.

Continue working straight until work measures 48 [50]cm, 18¾ [19½]in. Cast off.

Collar pieces: Work 2. With No 4½mm needles, cast on 42 sts in blue and work in K1, P1 rib for 20cm (8in) foll stripe sequence. Cast off.

Making up:
See page 7 for pressing and joining seams. Join seams. Turn in and stitch down knitted band at back of neck; stitch collar pieces in place, right over left, and crochet round outside edges with 1 row sl st in blue.

MAN'S JUMPER
Sizes:
102–107cm and 112–117cm (40–42in and 44–46in). Figures in square brackets [ ] refer to second size.

Materials:
700 [800]g yarn in dark blue, 100 [100]g in white.

Working instructions:
Back: With No 4½mm needles, cast on 90 [98] sts in blue and work 13 rows K1, P1 rib, foll stripe sequence.
Continue working in st st in blue on No 5mm needles until work measures 49cm (19¼in).
Shape armholes by casting off 7 sts at beg of next 2 rows = 76 [82] sts. Continue working straight until work measures 70 [72]cm, 27½ [28¼]in.
Shape shoulders by casting off 21 [24] sts at beg of next 2 rows. On rem 34 sts (right side of work) P 1 row, then work 3cm (1in) in st st for back neckband. Cast off.
Front: Work as for back until work measures 49 [49]cm, 19¼ [19¼]in.
Shape armholes as on back, then shape neck: *next row:* work 21 [24] sts, cast off 34, work to end. Continue on each group of sts until work measures 70 [72]cm, 27½ [28¼]in. Cast off.
Sleeves: With No 4½mm needles, cast on 48 [54] sts in blue and work 13 rows in K1, P1 rib, foll stripe sequence.
Continue working in st st in blue on No 5mm needles, inc 1 st at each end of every 8th row 11 times = 70 [76] sts.
Continue working straight until work measures 53 [55]cm, 21 [21¾]in. Cast off.
Collar: With No 4½mm needles, cast on 52 st in blue and work in K1, P1 rib for 22cm (8½in), foll stripe sequence.

Making up:
As for woman's jumper, but sew collar ends left over right.

CHILD'S JUMPER

Sizes:
To fit chest 66 and 76cm (27 and 30in).

Materials:
400 [450]g yarn in light blue, 50 [50]g in white.

Working instructions:
Back: With No 4½mm needles, cast on 62 [68] sts in blue and work in K1, P1 rib for 13 rows, foll stripe sequence.
Continue working in st st in blue on No 5mm needles until work measures 33cm (11in).
Shape armholes by casting off 5 sts at beg of next 2 rows = 52 [58] sts. Continue working straight until work measures 49 [50]cm, 19¼ [19½]in.
Shape shoulders by casting off 16 [19] sts at each end of next 2 rows. On rem 20 sts (right side of work) P 1 row, then work 2cm (¾in) in st st. Cast off.

Front: Work as for back until work measures 30 [32]cm, 11¾ [12½]in.
Shape neck: *next row:* work 16 [19] sts, cast off 20, work to end. Continue on each group of sts until work measures 49 [50]cm, 19¼ [19½]in. Cast off.
Sleeves: With No 4½mm needles, cast on 34 [40] sts in blue and work 11 rows in K1, P1 rib, foll stripe sequence.
Continue working in st st in blue on No 5mm needles, inc 1 st at each end of every 8th and 10th row alternately 7 times = 48 [54] sts.
Work straight until work measures 38 [40]cm, 15 [15¾]in. Cast off.
Collar: With No 4½mm needles, cast on 32 sts in blue, work in K1, P1 rib, foll stripe sequence, for 18cm (7in).

Making up:
See woman's jumper, but sew collar ends left over right.

The rugged look

A man's favourite type of knitted sweater: simple design, plenty of width for comfort, basically classic but with good fashion detail. The eye-catching feature of the long sleeved pullover is the band of ribbing on the sleeve. The sleeveless version makes a modern tank top.

BOTH GARMENTS
Sizes:
To fit chest 102–110cm and 112–117cm (40–42in and 44–46in).
Figures in square brackets [ ] refer to second size.

Materials:
Standard double knitting yarn. 1 pair each knitting needles No 3½mm and 4mm (UK sizes 9 and 7); 1 No 3½mm (UK size 9) circular twin-pin needle, 60 cm (24in) long.

Tension:
16 sts and 26 rows = 10cm (4in).

LONG-SLEEVED JERSEY
Materials:
600 [650]g yarn.

Working instructions:
Back: With No 3½mm needles, cast on 84 [90] sts and work 10cm (4in) in K2, P2 rib.
Change to No 4½mm needles and continue in garter st until work measures 36cm (14in).
Shape armholes by casting off 3 sts at beg of every row 4 times = 72 [78] sts. Now inc 1 st at each end of 4th row foll, then on every foll 8th row 10 times = 94 [100] sts. Continue straight until work measures 61 [62]cm, 24 [24½]in.
Shape shoulders by casting off 3 sts at beg of next 4 rows. Next row: cast off 3 sts (1 st on needle after cast off) patt 28 [31], cast off 18 sts, patt to end. Next row: cast off 3 sts (1 st on needle after cast off) patt 28 [31], turn.
Continue on each group of sts, casting off at armhole edge on alt rows, 3 sts once, 7 [8] sts twice; at the same time cast off 2 sts at neck edge on next and alt row, then dec 1 st at neck edge on foll alt row. Cast off rem 7 [8] sts.
Front: Work as for back until work measures 30 [31]cm, 11¾ [12¼]in.
Next row: patt 42 [45] sts, turn. Work on each group of sts, dec 1 st at neck edge on every 4th and 6th row alternately 8 times, then every 10th row 6 times; at the same time, when work measures 36cm (14in), shape armholes as on back. Complete as for back.
Sleeves: With No 3½mm needles, cast on 100 sts and work 10cm (4in) in K2, P2 rib.
Change to No 4½mm needles and work in garter st, knitting together on 1st row the 1st and 2nd sts, then the 2nd and 3rd foll sts alternately = 60 sts. Inc 1 st at each end of every 14th row 10 times [inc 1 st at each end of every 12th and 14th row alternately 11 times] = 80 [82] sts. Continue straight until work measures 51cm (20in).

Change to No 3½mm needles and work in K2, P2 rib inc alternately in every 2nd and 3rd st on 1st row = 132 [136] sts. When work measures 55cm (21½in), cast off loosely in rib.
Neckband: Using twin-pin needle, cast on 236 sts. Work in rounds in K2, P2 rib. On 1st round, mark 2 sts for V of neckline with coloured yarn and then on every round K first of these K sts tog with st immediately before it, and 2nd K st with st foll it. After 8 dec rounds have been worked, cast off all sts on next round.

Making up:
See page 7 for pressing and joining seams. Join seams, stitching lower 10cm (4in) of sleeve on right side for turn-up of cuff. Stitch neckband in place.

TANK TOP
Materials:
300 [350]g yarn.

Working instructions:
Back, front and neckband: Work as for long-sleeved jersey.
Armhole edging: With No 3½mm needles, cast on 94 sts and work 4cm (1½in) in K2, P2 rib; cast off loosely in rib.

Making up:
See page 7 for pressing and joining seams. Join seams. Stitch armhole edgings in place.

Mother and baby team

These two jumpers, knitted in a colourful zig-zag pattern, are just the thing for mother and child. The straight stripes on the sleeves are in the same colours as the zig-zag bands. Neckband and welt are worked in rib. An extra bonus for the toddler is the matching cap.

FOR BOTH MODELS
Materials:
Standard double knitting yarn. 1 pair each knitting needles Nos 3½mm and 4mm (UK sizes 9 and 8).

Tension over st st:
20 sts and 26 rows = 10cm (4in).

WOMAN'S JUMPER
Sizes:
To fit bust 76–81cm and 86–91cm (30–32in and 34–36in).
Figures in square brackets [ ] refer to second size.

Materials:
350 [400]g yarn in white, 50 [50]g each in blue, green, pink, yellow, red. Knitting needles as above plus 1 circular twin-pin needle No 3½mm (UK size 9), 40cm (16in) long.

Zig-zag pattern:
Stitches in multiples of 12 + 3.
1st row (right side): K1, *K4, slip 1 K2 tog, psso, K4, K into front, back and front of next st (i.e. K3 into same st), rep from * to last 2 sts, K2.
2nd row (wrong side): P. *3rd and 4th rows*: as 1st and 2nd. *5th–7th rows*: rep 1st and 2nd rows once, then 1st row again. *8th row*: K. *9th row*: as 1st row. *10th row*: K. Rep rows 1–10.

Stripe sequence:
6 rows blue, 4 rows white, 6 rows green, 4 rows white, 6 rows pink, 4 rows white, 6 rows yellow, 4 rows white, 6 rows red, 4 rows white.

Working instructions:
Back: With No 3½mm needles cast on 90 [101] sts in white and work in K1, P1 rib for 10cm (4in), then work 1 wrong-side row in purl, inc in 5th st and then every 10th st 8 [9] times = 99 [111] sts.
Change to No 4mm needles and work in zig-zag patt, first working 5th–10th rows in white, then working 1st–10th rows 5 times in stripe sequence as given; at the same time on last 9th row on every alt [on every] zig-zag point work only twice instead of 3 times into st; work thus 4 [8] times = 95 [103] sts.
Continue working straight in st st in white until work measures 61 [62]cm, 24 [24½]in.
Shape neck: *next row:* work across 69 [73] sts, slip the last 43 of these 69 [73] sts just worked on to a holder and leave, work to end.
Continue on each group of 26 [30] sts until work measures 65 [66]cm, 25½ [26]in. Cast off.

Front: Work as for back until work measures 51 [52]cm, 20 [20½]in. Slip centre 43 sts for neck on to holder as on back and complete as for back.
Sleeves: With No 3½mm needles cast on 37 [39] sts in white and work in K1, P1 rib for 10cm (4in).
Change to No 4mm needles and work 4 rows in garter st in white, inc on 1st row in every st except first and last sts = 72 [76] sts.
Now work stripe sequence of 50 rows once, working 6 coloured rows in st st, 4 white rows in garter st.
Continue in st st until work measures 40 [42]cm, 15¾ [16½]in. Inc 1 st at each end of next row, then on every alt row 9 more times = 92 [96] sts. Cast off loosely.

Making up:
Join seams. Using your circular needle and white yarn, slip 43 sts from holder at back on to needle, pick up 35 sts from 1st side to front holder, slip 43 sts from front holder on to needle, pick up 35 sts from 2nd side = 156 sts. Marking 1 K st in each corner with coloured yarn on 1st round, and working 3 sts tog with marked st in centre at these points on every alt round, work in K1, P1 rib for 4cm (1½)in.

CHILD'S JUMPER
Sizes:
To fit 56 [61]cm, 22 [24]in chest.
Figures in square brackets [ ] refer to second size.

Materials:
200 [250]g yarn in white, 50 [50]g each in 5 colours as for woman's jumper. Needles as above plus 2 sets double pointed needles in sizes 3½mm and 4mm (UK sizes 9 and 8).

Zig-zag pattern:
Stitches in multiples of 8 + 3.
1st row (right side): K1, *K2, slip 1, K2 tog, psso, K2, K into front, back and front of next st (i.e. K3 into same st), rep from * to last 2 sts, K2.
2nd row (wrong side): P. *3rd–5th rows*: rep 1st and 2nd rows once, then 1st row again.
6th row: K. *7th row*: as 1st row. *8th row*: K. Rep rows 1–8.

Stripe sequence:
4 rows each in blue, white, green, white, pink, white, yellow, white, red, white.

Working instructions:
Back: With No 3½mm needles, cast on 54 [60] sts in white and work 3cm (1in) in K1, P1 rib, then work one wrong-side row in purl, inc in every 10th [8th] st 5 [7] times = 59 [67] sts.
Change to No 4mm needles and work in zig-zag design, working 3rd–8th rows in white once, then working 1st–8th rows 5 times in stripe sequence as given; at the same time, in the last 7th row on every 2nd [on every] zig-zag point, work only 2 instead of 3 sts into the same st; work thus 3 [7] times = 56 [60] sts.
Continue working in white st st until work measures 28 [32]cm, 11 [12½]in.

Shape neck: *next row:* work across 40 [42] sts, slip the last 24 of these 40 [42] sts just worked on to a holder and leave, work to end. Continue on each group of 16 [18] sts until work measures 31 [35]cm, 12¼ [13¾]in. Cast off.

Front: Work as for back until work measures 25 [29]cm, 10 [11½]in, slip 24 centre sts on to a holder for neck and complete as for back.

Sleeves: With No 3½mm needles, cast on 28 [30] sts in white and work 3cm [1in] in K1, P1 rib.

Change to No 4mm needles and work in garter st, inc on 1st row in every alt st except for first and last sts: 12 [14] inc = 40 [44] sts.

Now work stripe sequence once, working coloured rows in st st and white rows in garter st.

Continue in st st until work measures 16 [20]cm, 6¼ [7¾]in. Inc 1 st at each end of next row, then on every alt row 3 times = 48 [52] sts. Cast off loosely.

Making up:
See page 7 for pressing and joining seams. Join seams. With set of No 3½mm needles and white yarn, slip 24 sts from back holder on to needle, pick up 17 sts from 1st side to front holder, slip 24 sts from front holder on to needle, then pick up 17 sts from 2nd side; work 3cm (1in) in K1, P1 rib, working corners as for woman's jumper.

CHILD'S CAP

With set of No 3½mm needles cast on 96 sts in white; working in rounds, work 3cm (1in) in K1, P1 rib.

Change to set of No 4mm needles and work first 20 rounds in stripe sequence as for sleeves, then work in st st in white. When work measures 10cm (4in), mark every 12th st with coloured yarn, then work the marked sts tog with sts lying before them on every alt round 6 times, then on every round 4 times. Break yarn, thread through rem sts; fasten off.

Cable matchmates

The thick cable twist on these two patterns makes them particularly attractive. The boy's sweater (which would look good on a little girl, too) has a polo neck; the dress has a plain skirt, worked in stocking stitch.

BOTH GARMENTS
Sizes:
To fit chest 61–64cm (24–26in).

Materials:
Aran-type double knitting yarn. 1 pair each knitting needles Nos 4½mm and 5mm (UK sizes 7 and 6); 1 set of No 4½mm (UK size 7) needles pointed at both ends; 1 cable needle.

Tension over Aran pattern:
24 sts and 26 rows = 10cm (4in).

Aran pattern:
1st and all following wrong-side rows: *K2, P4, K2, P6, rep from *, then K2, P4, K2.
2nd row (right side): *P2, cross 2 to right (K 2nd st in front of 1st st, then K 1st st behind it), cross 2 to left (K 2nd st behind 1st st, then K 1st st in front of it), P2, K2, cable 4 sts to right (slip 2 sts on cable needle and place behind work, K next 2 sts, then K2 from cable needle), rep from *; at end of row P2, cross 2 to right, cross 2 to left, P2.
4th row: *P2, cross 2 sts to left, cross 2 sts to right, P2, K6, rep from *; at end of row P2, cross 2 to left, cross 2 to right, P2.
6th row: *P2, cross 2 to right, cross 2 to left, P2, cable 4 to left (slip 2 sts on cable needle and place in front of work, K next 2 sts, then K2 from cable needle), K2, rep from *; at end of row P2, cross 2 to right, cross 2 to left, P2.
8th row: as 4th row. Rep 1st to 8th rows.

Welt stitch:
K1, P1 rib.

SWEATER
Materials:
350g yarn.

Working instructions:
Back: With No 4½mm needles, cast on 78 sts and work 6cm (2¼in) in K1, P1 rib.
Change to No 5mm needles and work straight in Aran patt until work measures 27cm (10¾in).
Shape armholes as follows: cast off 3 sts at beg of next 2 rows, then 2 sts at beg of foll 2 rows; then dec 1 st at each end of foll 2 alt rows = 64 sts. Work straight until work measures 40cm (15½in).
Shape neck and shoulders. *Next row:* patt 23, cast off 18, patt to end.
Continue on each group of sts by casting off 3 sts at neck edge on foll alt row. *Next row:* cast off 9, patt to end. *Next row:* Cast off 2, patt to end. Cast off rem 9 sts.

Front: Work as for back until work measures 36cm (14in). Shape neck and shoulders: *next row:* patt 29, cast off 6, patt to end.
Continue on each group of sts, casting off at neck edge on foll alt rows, 3 sts once, 2 sts twice, then dec 1 st at neck edge on every alt row 3 times. *Next row:* cast off 9, patt to end. *Next row:* work 2 tog, patt to end. Cast off rem 9 sts.
Sleeves: With No 4½mm needles, cast on 38 sts and work 12cm (4¾in), in K1, P1 rib.
Change to No 5mm needles and work in Aran patt, positioning cable stripe up centre, thus 1st row will read: *K2, P6, K2, P4, rep from * once, K2, P6, K2. Inc 1 st at each end of every 6th row 10 times = 58 sts.
Continue straight until work measures 36cm (14in). Shape top of sleeve as follows: cast off 3 sts at beg of next 4 rows, 2 sts at beg of next 16 rows, 3 sts at beg of foll 2 rows. Cast off rem sts.

Making up:
See page 7 for pressing and joining seams. Join shoulder seams. Using set of needles, pick up 78 sts from neck and work in rounds for 12cm (4¾in) in K1, P1 rib, cast off loosely. Join seams, turning bottom 5cm (2in) of sleeves to right side for turn-up cuffs.

DRESS
Materials:
400g yarn. Needles as for sweater plus 1 circular twin-pin needle No 5mm (UK size 6), 80cm long.

Tension over stocking stitch:
18 sts and 26 rounds (rows) = 10cm (4in).

Working instructions:
Skirt: With the circular needle, cast on 172 sts and work for 3cm (1in) in K1, P1 rib. Continue working in st st until work measures 27cm (10½in), then K tog 8th and 9th then 7th and 8th sts and rep 20 times = 152 sts.
Now divide work at end of last round with 76 sts on each half of work.
First work *back* in Aran patt, with trellis rib up centre, thus 1st row will read: P6, *K2, P4, K2, P6; rep from * to end, and 6th row will start cable 4 left. Work straight until work measures 44cm (17¼in).
Work armholes as described for sweater omitting last dec row = 64 sts; when work measures 57cm (22½in), shape neck and shoulders as described for sweater but casting off 7 sts in place of 9 for shoulders.
Work *front*, shaping side seam, armholes and shoulders as for back. When work measures 53cm (21in), shape neck as for front of sweater.
Sleeves: With No 4½mm needles, cast on 38 sts, work 6cm (2¼in) in K1, P1 rib.
Change to No 5mm needles and work in Aran patt, foll patt rows as given, and working side inc and top of sleeve when work measures 30cm (11¾in), as for sweater.

Making up:
As for sweater, but work neckband only 3cm (1in) deep.

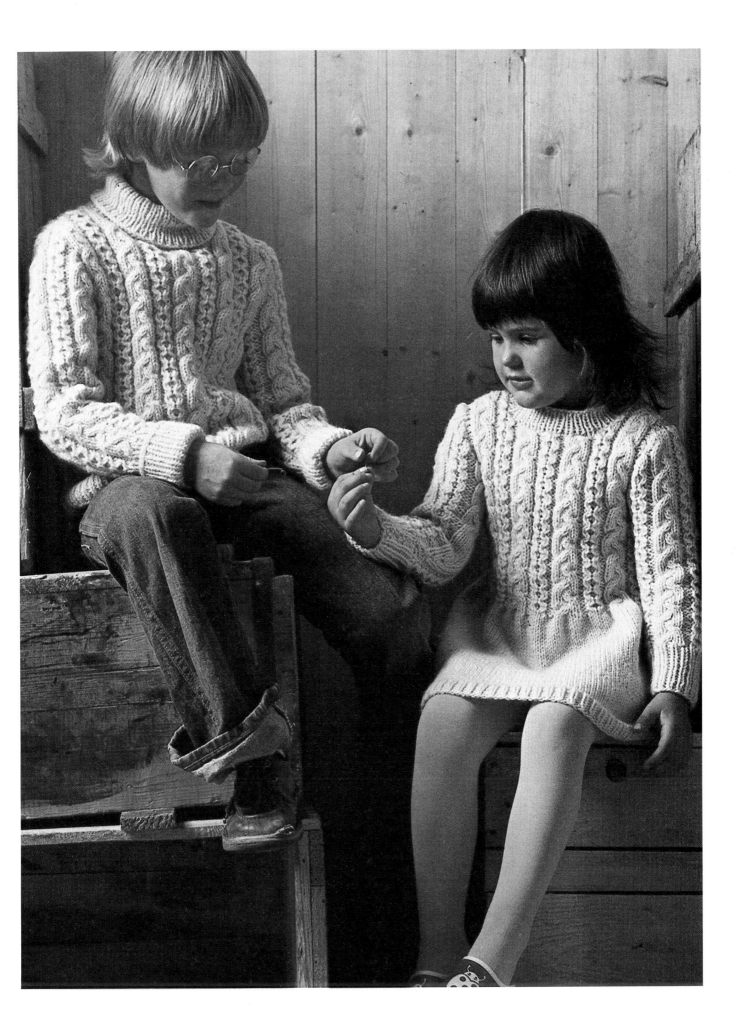

Winter glamour

This long trendy scarf is knitted in single ribbing with colour-pattern insets in double thickness lying at front of the neck; each section is knitted separately and then joined together. In the colour insets, stripes are knitted in and diamond motifs are embroidered on the knitting, but you can knit them in if you prefer. Add long fringes for extra dash. Smart, close-fitting cap and snug gloves complete the picture.

Sizes:
Cap: To fit average head. **Gloves:** size $6\frac{1}{2}$–7.

Materials:
Standard double knitting yarn; 1 pair knitting needles No $3\frac{1}{2}$mm (UK size 9); 1 set of 4 double-pointed needles No $3\frac{1}{2}$mm (UK size 9) and 1 spare double-pointed needle No $3\frac{1}{2}$mm (UK size 9); 1 crochet hook.

Stripe sequence:
1 row yellow, 2 rows dark green, 9 rows brown, 2 rows dark green, 1 row yellow, 2 rows brown, in both these rows slipping every 4th yellow st and carrying yarn across back of work, 1 row red, 2 rows lilac, slipping every 4th red st and spacing between yellow sts, 1 row red, 2 rows brown, 1 row yellow, 2 rows dark green = 26 rows.

Embroidered pattern:
1 patt rep across is shown on chart. Cross = 1 st in corresponding colour, blank squares = knitted background. See page 8 for instructions on how to work embroidery on knitting.

Tension over colour patt in st st:
22 sts and 30 rows or rounds = 10cm (4in).

SCARF
Materials:
200g brown yarn; oddments dark green, yellow, red, lilac and light green.

Working instructions:
For scarf 18cm (7in) wide. With No $3\frac{1}{2}$mm needles, cast on 68 sts and slipping first st on every row work in K1, P1 rib until work measures 38cm (15in). *Next row:* sl first st onto spare needle, *K1, sl next st on same spare needle, rep from * to end = 34 sts on each needle. Leave sts on spare needle and work on first set in st st, inc in every 4th st on first row 7 times = 41 sts.
Work for 4cm ($1\frac{1}{2}$in) in brown, then work stripe sequence once, work 4 cm ($1\frac{1}{2}$in) more in brown, dec 7 times across the last row. Leave these 34 sts on spare needle.
Slip the 34 sts left on first spare needle onto No $3\frac{1}{2}$mm needle and work to match first set.
Now join sts again by working 1 st from each needle alternately = 68 sts and work in K1, P1 rib slipping first st on every row.

When work measures 75cm ($29\frac{1}{2}$in), centre of scarf has been reached.
Work other half of scarf to match, reversing stripe sequence. Cast off (work should now measure 150cm (59in)).

Making up:
Work 1 row dc in brown along st st edges. Embroider brown areas of stripe sequence with diamond motif as shown on embroidery chart. Make fringe for ends of scarf: cut strands of brown wool 20cm (8in) long and knot 4 strands at a time into ends of work.

CAP
Materials:
50g ball brown yarn; oddments of coloured yarns as for scarf.

Working instructions:
Using set of 4 needles, cast on 112 sts in brown and work 3cm (1in) in rounds.
Continue in st st, working stripe sequence once.
Continue working in brown, marking every 14th st 8 times on first round for dec. In foll round, K2 tog before marked sts, then K2 tog after marked sts = 96 sts.
Continue dec in this way on every 3rd round 4 times more = 32 sts, then on 2nd foll round K tog 3 sts lying between marked points. On rem 16 sts, work 2 more rounds. Break yarn, thread through rem sts. Draw up and fasten off securely. Embroider diamond motifs, following chart above, as described for scarf.

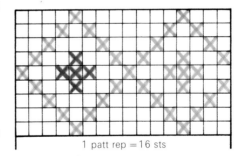

1 patt rep = 16 sts

GLOVES
Materials:
50g ball brown yarn; oddments of coloured yarn as for scarf.

Working instructions:
Using set of 4 needles and 1 spare double-pointed needle, cast on 40 sts (10 sts on each needle) in brown and work in K1, P1 rib in rounds for 10cm (4in).

Now work in st st as follows: 1 round brown, then work stripe sequence once, beg inc for thumb on the 3rd round; for right-hand glove, pick up loop knitwise after first st on first needle, for left-hand glove pick up loop knitwise before last st on 4th needle. Continue inc 1 st each side of this inc on every 3rd round 7 times more = 55 sts. After 23 rounds in st st are completed leave 15 sts for thumb on a holder, cast on 5 sts with a guiding thread at base of thumb, work 45 sts straight; at the same time K tog first st at base of thumb with preceding st and last st at base of thumb with foll st twice on every 2nd round. K tog last st rem at base of thumb with sts on either side = 40 sts. At end of stripe sequence work in brown. After 5 rounds in brown work little finger: pick up 5 sts each from back and front of hand, casting on 2 sts for join with next finger and inserting a marking thread = 12 sts. Divide on 3 needles and work straight for 5cm (2in).

Shape top: K tog last 2 sts on every needle on next 3 rounds. Break yarn, draw through rem 3 sts and fasten off securely. Remove marking thread from 2 joining sts and work 2 rounds over all sts.

Work ring finger: pick up 4 sts each from back and front of hand, plus 2 sts from join with little finger and cast on 2 more sts for join with middle finger = 12 sts. Work for 7cm (2¾in), then work finger top as for little finger.

For middle finger, pick up 5 sts each side of hand and 2 sts for join at each side of finger = 14 sts, then work as for ring finger.

Work index finger with the rem 12 sts plus 2 sts for join = 14 sts; work 6cm (2¼in), complete top, dec as for little finger.

Finally work the thumb: pick up sts left on holder, remove marking thread from base of thumb, pick up 5 sts and K over all 20 sts, dec newly picked-up sts as for base of thumb on hand part. When thumb measures 5cm (2in) complete top, dec as for little finger.

Embroider brown area of stripe sequence, beg after base of thumb, where only one small green diamond is worked.

Partners in contrast

Sweaters to match with the same Fair Isle type of design. The woman's jersey has a round neck and the man's a straight neck. Clever colour switch makes them complement each other.

FOR BOTH SWEATERS
Materials:
Standard 4 ply yarn. 1 pair each knitting needles Nos 2½mm and 3mm (UK sizes 12 and 11).

Tension:
Working coloured design in st st: 29 sts and 36 rows = 10cm (4in).

WOMAN'S SWEATER
Sizes:
76–81cm and 86–91cm (30–32in and 34–36in).
Figures in square brackets [ ] refer to second size.

Materials:
350 [400]g in navy blue and 100 [100]g in grey. As above plus 1 circular twin-pin needle No 2½mm (UK size 12), 40cm (16in) long.

Colour design:
Chart shows 1 patt rep across + end st. Rep rows 1 to 56, working squares containing crosses in grey, blank squares in navy blue = background colour. (Each square = 1 st.)
NB: K first and last st on every row (referred to as edge sts). These 2 sts are not shown on the colour chart.

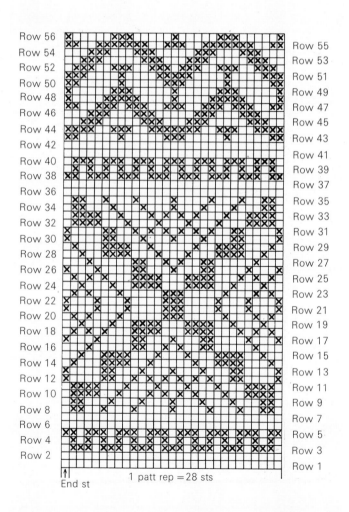

1 patt rep = 28 sts

End st

84

Back: With No 2½mm needles, cast on 104 [114] sts in navy blue and work for 12cm (4¾in) in K1, P1 rib.

Continue working with No 3mm needles in patt, foll chart and inc on first row in 8th [9th] st, then on every 4th st another 22 [24] times = 127 [139] sts. Work 2nd row of chart, then on 3rd row K edge st, beg the colour patt from chart with the 23rd [17th] st of the 28 st rep, then work the 28 st rep 4 times. Work to the 6th [12th] st of the 28 st rep, then work end st as on chart; K edge st. Continue working from chart on sts as placed until work measures 34cm (13½in).

Shape armholes by casting off 5 sts at beg of next 2 rows, 2 sts at beg of next 8 rows, then dec 1 st at each end of every alt row 4 times = 93 [105] sts.

Continue working straight until work measures 52 [53]cm, 20½ [21]in.

Shape neck and shoulders: *next row:* patt 26 [32], cast off 41, patt to end. Continue on each group of sts by casting off 5 [7] sts at beg of next and foll 2 alt rows; at the same time cast off 2 sts at neck edge on foll 2 alt rows, then dec 1 st at neck edge on foll alt row. Cast off rem 6 sts.

Front: Work as for back until work measures 45 [46]cm, 17¾ [18]in.

Shape neck: *next row:* patt 41 [47], cast off 11, patt to end. Now cast off 3 sts at neck edge on foll 3 alt rows, then dec 1 st at same edge on every alt row 6 times. Continue straight until work measures 52 [53]cm, 20½ [21]in, then complete as for back.

Sleeves: With No 2½mm needles, cast on 52 [58] sts in blue, work 8cm (3in) in K1, P1 rib. Change to No 3mm needles and work in navy st st, inc 1 st at each end of work on every 6th and 8th rows alt 16 times = 84 [90] sts. Continue straight until work measures 43 [44]cm, 17 [17¼]in.

Shape top of sleeve by casting off at beg of every row 3 sts twice, 2 sts 8 times, then dec 1 st at each end of every alt row 13 [15] times. Now cast off at beg of every row 2 sts 6 times, 3 sts 4 times. Cast off rem 12 [14] sts.

Making up:
See page 7 for pressing and joining seams. Join seams. With the circular needle, pick up 130 sts in blue round neck and work 3cm (1in) in K1, P1 rib. Cast off loosely in rib.

MAN'S SWEATER
Sizes:
To fit chest 97–102cm and 107–112cm (38–40in and 42–44in).
Figures in square brackets [ ] refer to second size.

Materials:
450 [500]g in grey, 150 [150]g in navy blue.

Colour design:
As for woman's jersey but work squares with crosses in navy blue and blank squares in grey.
NB: K first and last st on every row.
Back: With No 2mm needles, cast on 143 [155] sts and work 8cm (3in) in K1, P1 rib.
Continue in patt on same needles and work 2 rows from chart, then on 3rd row K edge st, beg the colour patt from

chart with the 15th [9th] st of the 28 st rep, then work the 28 st rep 4 times. Work to the 20th [13th] st of the 28 st rep, then work end st as on chart; K edge st. Continue working from chart on sts as placed until work measures 42cm (16½in). Shape armholes by casting off 6 sts at beg of next 2 rows, 2 sts at beg of next 8 rows, then dec 1 st at each end of every alt row 5 times = 105 [117] sts. Continue working straight until work measures 64 [65] cm, 25 [25½]in.

Shape neck: *next row:* patt 32, cast off 41 [53], patt to end. Continue on each group of sts, casting off at neck edge on foll alt rows 3 sts once, 2 sts twice, then dec 1 st at same edge on every alt row twice, every 2nd and 4th rows alt 14 times. *At the same time* when work measures 66 [67]cm, 26 [26½]in, inc 1 st at shoulder edge once, then inc 1 st on every 2nd and 4th rows alt 11 times more. When work measures 76 [77]cm, 30 [30½]in, cast off 2 sts on every alt row 9 times, 3 sts once.

Front: Work as for back until work measures 56 [57]cm, 22 [22½]in. With No 2½mm needles, work 3cm (1in) in K1, P1 rib in grey, cast off.

Sleeves: With No 2½mm needles, cast on 66 [72] sts in grey and work 8cm (3in) in K1, P1 rib.
Change to No 3mm needles and work in grey st st inc 1 st at each end of every 8th and 10th rows alt 16 times = 98 [104] sts. Continue working straight until work measures 50cm (19¾in).

Shape top of sleeve by casting off at beg of every row 3 sts twice [4 times], 2 sts 10 [8] times, then dec 1 st at each end of every alt row 15 times. Now cast off at beg of every row 2 sts 8 times, 3 sts 4 times, then cast off rem 14 [18] sts.

Making up:
See page 7 for pressing and joining seams. With No 2½mm needles pick up 159 [169] sts in grey from back of neck and work 3cm (1in) in K1, P1 rib, cast off loosely in rib. Stitch yoke to front neckband. Join all other seams.

In classic style

Simplicity is good fashion and these two cardigans suit all age groups. They are worked in a special rib pattern, with practical pockets, plus a small breast pocket on the man's cardigan.

BOTH GARMENTS
Materials:
Standard double knitting yarn. 1 pair each knitting needles Nos 3mm and 3½mm (UK sizes 11 and 9); 1 circular twin-pin needle No 3mm (UK size 11), 80cm (30in) long; 5 buttons.

Tension:
22 sts and 33 rows = 10cm (4in).

WOMAN'S CARDIGAN
Sizes:
To fit bust 86–91cm and 97–102cm (34–36in and 38–40in). Figures in square brackets [ ] refer to second size.

Materials:
500 [550]g yarn.

Main Pattern:

1st row (right-side row): K1, *P7, K1, P3, K1, rep from * to last 8 sts, P7, K1.

2nd row (wrong-side row): K1, then K all P sts and P all K sts from previous row to last st, K1.

3rd row: K1, *P7, K1 into st on row below, P3, K1 below; rep from * to last 8 sts, P7, K1. Rep 2nd and 3rd rows.

Working instructions:

Back: With No 3mm needles, cast on 109 [117] sts and work 4cm (1½in) in K1, P1 rib.

Change to No 3½mm needles and work in patt as follows. First size, *next row*: K1, P3, K1, *P7, K1, P3, K1, rep from * to last 8 sts, P7, K1. Second size, *next row*: work as 1st row of patt.

Continue in patt dec 1 st at each end of every 8th row 7 times = 95 [103] sts. Now inc 1 st at each end of every 8th row 5 times = 105 [113] sts.

When work measures 42 [43]cm, 16½ [17]in, shape armholes as follows: cast off 4 sts at beg of next 2 rows, 2 sts at beg of next 4 [6] rows, then dec 1 st at each end of every alt row 5 times = 79 [83] sts. Continue working straight until work measures 61 [63]cm, 24 [25]in.

Shape neck and shoulders as follows: *next row*: patt 27 [29], cast off 25 sts, patt to end.

Work across each group of sts by casting off 5 [6] sts at armhole edge and 2 sts at neck edge on next and foll alt row. Now cast off 6 [6] sts at armhole edge and dec 1 st at neck edge on foll alt row. Cast off.

Left front: With No 3mm needles, cast on 53 [57] sts and work 4cm (1½in) in K1, P1 rib.

Change to No 3½mm needles and continue working in patt (working 2 sts less at beg and end of every patt row on first size only), shaping side, armhole and shoulder as for back.

When work measures 14cm (5½in), slip 12th to 44th [16th to 48th] sts from front edge on a holder for pocket and leave.

Work to end of row.

Cast on 33 sts and work in patt for 10cm (4in), then working back across left front, work the 33 pocket-lining sts in place of sts left on holder.

When work measures 35cm (13¾in), work dart as follows: leave 5 [4] sts unworked at right-hand edge on a wrong-side row, yrn, turn, then on foll wrong-side rows leave 5 [4] more sts unworked 4 [6] times. Finally work across all sts, working yrn tog with st lying beside it each time.

When work measures 38cm (15in), dec at front edge for neck as follows: 1 st once, then on every 6th row 1 st 15 times more.

Pick up sts left on holder and work pocket top as follows: K1 right-side row, then working in K1, P1 rib work 13 rows. Cast off.

Right front: Work to match left front reversing shapings.

Sleeves: With No 3mm needles, cast on 57 [57] sts, work in K1, P1 rib for 13 rows.

Change to No 3½mm needles and continue working in patt as follows. First size, as left front. Second size: as 1st row of patt. Inc 1 st at each end of every 10th row 13 times = 83 [83] sts. Continue straight until work measures 45cm (17¾in).

Shape top of sleeve by casting off at beg of every row 4 sts twice, 2 sts 8 [8] times, then dec 1 st at each end of every alt row 13 [13] times. Now cast off at beg of every row 2 sts 8 times, 4 sts twice. Cast off rem 9 sts.

Edging: With the circular needle, cast on 359 [371] sts for the entire length. Work 13 rows in K1, P1 rib, slipping 1st st of every row; at the same time work buttonholes in 5th row by casting off 3 sts for each buttonhole and casting on 3 sts on return row. Work 1st buttonhole 1.5cm (½in) from bottom right edge and 4 more at intervals of 7.5cm (3in).

Making up:

Stitch sides of pocket top ribbing neatly in position. Stitch pocket lining in position at back of neck. See page 7 for pressing and joining seams. Pin front band carefully in place all round front edges, then stitch neatly in position. Join seams. Sew on buttons to match buttonholes.

MAN'S CARDIGAN

Sizes:

To fit chest 97–102cm and 107–112cm (38–40in and 42–44in). Figures in square brackets [ ] refer to second size.

Materials:

550 [600]g yarn.

Main pattern:

1st row (right-side row): K1, *P5, K1, rep from * to last 6 sts, P5, K1.

2nd row (wrong-side row): K1, then K all purl sts and P all knit sts from previous row to last st, K1.

3rd row: K1, *P5, K1 working into st on row below, repeat from * to last 6 sts, P5, K1. Rep 2nd and 3rd rows.

Working instructions:

Back: With No 3mm needles, cast on 115 [121] sts, work 6cm (2½in) in K1, P1 rib.

Change to No 3½mm needles and continue working straight in patt until work measures 40cm (15¾in).

Shape armholes as follows: cast off at beg of every row 4 sts twice, 2 sts 6 times, then dec 1 st at each end of every alt row 4 [5] times = 87 [91] sts. Continue working straight until work measures 63 [64]cm, 24½ [25]in.

Shape neck and shoulders as follows: *next row:* patt 29 [31], cast off 29, patt to end. Work across each group of sts by casting off 6 [6] sts at armhole edge and 2 sts at neck edge on next and foll alt row. Now cast off 6 [7] sts at armhole edge and dec 1 st at neck edge on foll alt row. Cast off.

Left front: With No 3mm needles, cast on 55 [58] sts, work 6cm (2½in) in K1, P1 rib.

Change to No 3½mm needles and continue working in patt, shaping for armhole and shoulder as for back. When work measures 18cm (7in), slip 3rd to 35th sts from right-hand edge on a holder for pocket and leave. Work to end of row. Cast on 33 sts, work in patt for 12cm (4¾in); then working back across left front, work the 33 pocket-lining sts in place of sts left on holder. When work measures 40cm (15¾in), dec at left-hand edge for neck as follows: 1 st once, then on every 4th row dec 1 st 10 times, then on every 6th row 1 st 6 times; at the same time when work measures 50cm (19½in) place pockets: *next row:* patt 4, slip 5th to 27th sts from armhole edge on a holder for breast pocket and leave. Patt to end of row.

Cast on 23 sts, work 5cm (2in) in patt, then working across left front, work the 23 pocket-lining sts in place of sts left on holder. Pick up sts on holder for larger pocket and work pocket top in K1, P1 rib for 3.5cm (1½in); work pocket top of breast pocket for 2.5cm (1in) in K1, P1 rib.

Right front: Work to match left front, reversing shapings and omitting breast pocket.

Sleeves: With No 3mm needles, cast on 61 [67] sts and work 6cm (2½in) in K1, P1 rib.

Change to No 3½mm needles and continue in patt, inc 1 st at each end of every 12th row 11 times = 83 [89] sts. Continue straight until work measures 48cm (19in), then shape top of sleeve as follows: cast off at beg of every row 4 sts twice, 2 sts 6 times, then dec 1 st at each end of every alt row 17 [19] times.

Cast off at beg of every row 2 sts 6 times, 4 sts twice. Cast off rem 9 [11] sts.

Edging: With circular needle, cast on 327 [333] sts and work in rows in K1, P1 rib, slipping first st on every row for 4cm (1½in); at the same time work buttonholes 2cm (¾in) in from start of work by casting off 4 sts for each buttonhole and casting on 4 sts on return row. Work first buttonhole 2cm (¾in) from bottom left-hand edge, work 4 more at intervals of 7cm (2¾in).

Making up:
See woman's cardigan.

Easy as winking

Nothing could be simpler than the pattern for this pullover and cardigan, both knitted across from sleeve to sleeve in garter stitch stripes. The cardigan is knitted in one colour and the V-neck pullover in three toning colours and white. The V-neck pullover and open-fronted cardigan slip on easily and both have deep turn-up cuffs.

BOTH GARMENTS
Sizes:
To fit bust 81–86cm and 97–97cm (32–34in and 36–38in). Figures in square brackets [ ] refer to second size.

Materials:
Double double knitting yarn. 1 pair knitting needles No 6mm (UK size 4).

CARDIGAN
Materials:
700 [800]g yarn in natural.

Pattern:
*8 rows st st; 12 rows (6 ridges) garter st. Rep from *.

Tension:
13 sts and 22 rows = 10cm (4in).

Working instructions:
Cardigan is worked from sleeve to sleeve. Starting with the left sleeve, cast on 42 sts and work in garter st, beg with a wrong-side row, until work measures 17cm (6½in).
Continue in patt, beg with 12 rows st st and shaping as follows: inc 1 st at each end of next row and every 8th and 10th row alternately 8 times = 60 sts; inc 1 st at each end of every alt row 3 times, then cast on 2 sts at beg of next 4 rows. When work measures 55cm (21½in), cast on 42 [44] sts at beg of next 2 rows = 158 [162] sts.
Now work straight slipping first st on every row and working 10 sts at both edges in garter st and rem sts between in patt until work measures 80 [82]cm, 31½ [32¼]in, after 7th patt rep.
Cast off 79 [81] sts at left-hand edge for left front and cast them on again for right front on foll row, then complete second half of jacket to match.

Making up:
See page 7 for pressing and joining seams.
Join sleeve and side seams, stitching lower 10cm (4in) of sleeves on the right side for the cuffs.

PULLOVER
Materials:
200 [300]g yarn in rust, beige, blue and white.

Stripe sequence:
Cast on and work 9 rows in white, *10 rows (5 ridges) in each of the 4 colours, rep from *.

Tension:
13 sts and 26 rows = 10cm (4in).

Working instructions:
The pullover is worked in one piece. Starting at left sleeve, cast on 38 sts in white and work in patt, foll stripe sequence, inc 1 st at each end of every 10th row 10 times, then every alt row 7 times = 72 sts.
When work measures 45cm (17¾in), cast on 48 [50] sts at beg of next 2 rows = 168 [172] sts.
Continue working straight slipping first st on every row. After working 18 stripes [in middle of the 19th stripe], on a wrong-side row, work 52 [54] sts at front edge, cast off 40 sts for neck, work last 76 [78] sts. On the foll row, work 76 [78] sts, cast on 40 sts in colour of next stripe [in colour of same stripe], work 52 [54] sts.
Continue working second half of pullover to match, keeping stripe sequence correct and reversing shapings, i.e. inc becomes dec.

Making up:
Join sleeve and side seams.

Key:
each cross = 1 st

Colour chart shows 1 rep
across + end st

Row 15
Row 13
Row 11
Row 9
Row 7
Row 5
Row 3
Row 1

Row 14
Row 12
Row 10
Row 8
Row 6
Row 4
Row 2

1

End st
1 patt rep = 6 sts

Diamonds are trumps

Sweaters to match in a chunky diamond pattern. Country-style colours are misty green for hers and two shades of green with natural contrast for his.

BOTH GARMENTS
Materials:
Triple double knitting yarn. 1 pair each knitting needles Nos 7mm and 8mm (UK sizes 2 and 0); 1 set of No 7mm (UK size 2) needles pointed at both ends.

Pattern:
See chart, below right. 1 pattern repeat across plus end stitch is given. Rep rows 1–12.

Tension:
11 sts and 16 rows = 10cm (4in).

MAN'S SWEATER
Sizes:
To fit chest 102–107cm and 112–117cm (40–42in and 44–46in).
Figures in square brackets [ ] refer to second size.

Materials:
1000 [1100]g in dark green, 450 [500]g in white, 100 [150]g in flecked green.

Working instructions:
Back: With No 7mm needles, cast on 61 [65] sts in dark green and work 8cm (3¼in) in K1, P1 rib.
Change to No 8mm needles and continue working in patt, beg after working edge st with 2nd [10th] st of patt rep. When 4½ patt reps have been worked, work should measure 42cm (16½in).
Work 15 rows from colour patt chart, then continue in patt in light green beg with 10th patt row. When work measures 72 [73]cm, 28½ [28¾]in, shape neck as follows: *next row:* patt 23 [24], cast off 13 [15] patt to end. Now cast off at neck edge on each group of sts, 2 sts on next alt row, then dec 1 st on foll alt row. Cast off rem 20 [21] sts for shoulder.
Front: Work as for back until work measures 65 [66]cm, 25½ [26]in.
Shape neck as follows: *next row:* patt 28 [29], cast off 5 [7], patt to end. Now cast off at neck edge on each group of sts, 2 sts on every alt row twice, then dec 1 st on every alt row 4 times. Cast off rem 20 [21] sts for shoulder.
Sleeves: With No 7mm needles, cast on 33 [35] sts in dark green and work 8cm (3¼in) in K1, P1 rib.
Change to No 8mm needles and continue working in patt in dark green, beg after working edge st with 6th [3rd] st of patt rep. Inc 1 st at each end of every 6th row 9 times = 51 [53] sts; at the same time when 4 patt reps have been completed (work should measure 38cm (15in)), work the 15 rows from colour patt chart, then continue in patt in light green, beg with 10th row of patt.
When work measures 48cm (19in), after finishing colour patt, shape top of sleeve by casting off 3 sts at beg of next

2 rows, 4 sts at beg of foll 2 rows. Rep last 4 rows twice more. Cast off rem 9 [11] sts.
Neckband: With set of needles, cast on 68 [74] sts in light green and work in K1, P1 rib in rounds for 4cm (1½in). Cast off loosely in rib.

Making up:
See page 7 for pressing and joining seams. Join seams. Stitch cast-on edge of neckband to neck.

WOMAN'S SWEATER
Sizes:
To fit bust 86–91cm and 97–102cm (34–36in and 38–40in).
Figures in square brackets [ ] refer to second size.

Materials:
1300 [1400]g in light green.

Working instructions:
Back: With No 7mm needles, cast on 59 [63] sts and work 8cm (3¼in) in K1, P1 rib.
Change to No 8mm needles and continue working in patt, beg after working edge st with 4th [12th] st of patt rep.
When work measures 67cm (26½in), shape neck as follows: *next row:* patt 23 [24], cast off 13 [15], patt to end. Now cast off at neck edge on each group of sts, 2 sts on next alt row, then dec 1 st on foll alt row. Cast off rem 20 [21] sts for shoulder.
Front: Work as for back until work measures 61cm (24in). Shape neck as follows: *next row:* patt 27 [28], cast off 5 [7], patt to end. Now cast off at neck edge, 2 sts on every alt row twice, then dec 1 st on every alt row 3 times. Cast off rem 20 [21] sts for shoulder.
Sleeves: With No 7mm needles, cast on 27 [29] sts and work 8cm (3¼in) in K1, P1 rib.
Change to No 8mm needles and work in patt, beg after working edge st with 12th [10th] row of patt rep. Inc 1 st at each side of every 4th and 6th rows alt, 10 times = 47 [49] sts. When work measures 44 [45]cm, 17½ [17¾]in, shape top of sleeve by casting off 4 sts at beg of next 10 rows. Cast off rem 7 [9] sts.
Neckband: With set of needles, cast on 64 [70] sts and work in K1, P1 rib in rounds for 4cm (1½in). Cast off loosely in rib.

Making up:
See page 7 for pressing and joining seams. Join seams. Stitch cast-on edge of neckband to neck.

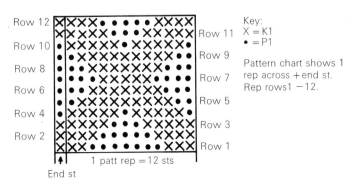

Polo-neck variations

These warm woollen sweaters are knitted to the same basic pattern, except for their different necks and sleeve lengths. One version has long sleeves and a close-fitting polo neck in rib. Another version has a big loose collar with horizontal ribbing and short sleeves and the third sweater has a loose-fitting polo collar and is sleeveless. Of course, you can mix sleeve length and style of neck to suit your own taste.

ALL GARMENTS
Sizes:
To fit bust 81–86cm and 91–97cm (32–34in and 36–38in). Figures in square brackets [ ] refer to second size.

Materials:
Standard 4-ply yarn. 1 pair each knitting needles Nos $2\frac{1}{2}$mm and 3mm (UK sizes 12 and 11). 1 circular twin-pin needle No $2\frac{1}{2}$mm (UK size 12), 40cm (16in) long.

Tension over stocking stitch:
28 sts and 40 rows = 10cm (4in).

LONG-SLEEVED SWEATER
Materials:
300 [350]g yarn.

Working instructions:
Back: With No $2\frac{1}{2}$mm needles, cast on 134 [144] sts and work in K1, P1 rib for 4cm ($1\frac{1}{2}$in).
Change to No 3mm needles and work in st st, dec 1 st at each end of every 8th row 10 times = 114 [124] sts. Now inc 1 st at each end of every 10th row 7 times = 128 [138] sts. Continue straight until work measures 44 [43]cm, $17\frac{1}{2}$ [17]in.
Shape for armholes as follows: cast off 6 sts at beg of next 2 rows, 2 sts at beg of foll 8 rows, then dec 1 st at both ends of every alt row 5 times = 90 [100] sts. Continue working straight until work measures 63cm ($24\frac{3}{4}$in).
Shape neck and shoulders: *next row*: K 30 [35] sts, cast off 30 sts, K to end. Continue on each group of sts as follows: cast off 6 [7] sts at armhole edge on next and foll 2 [1] alt rows, 8 sts at same edge of foll alt row on larger size only; at the same time cast off 2 sts at neck edge on next 2 alt rows, then dec 1 st at same edge of foll alt row. Cast off rem 7 [8] sts.
Front: Work as for back until work measures 58cm ($22\frac{3}{4}$in).
Shape neck: *next row*: K 39 [44] sts, cast off 12 sts, K to end. Continue on each group of sts by casting off 2 sts at neck edge on every alt row 4 times, then dec 1 st at same edge of every alt row 6 times. Shape shoulder as for back.
Sleeves: With No $2\frac{1}{2}$mm needles, cast on 60 [66] sts and work in K1, P1 rib for 4cm ($1\frac{1}{2}$in).
Change to No 3mm needles and work in st st, inc 1 st at each end of every 8th row 18 times = 96 [102] sts. Continue until work measures 42cm ($16\frac{1}{2}$in).
Shape top of sleeve as follows: cast off at beg of every row 4 sts twice, 2 sts 10 times, then dec 1 st at each end of every row 14 [16] times. Now cast off at beg of every row 2 sts 10 times, 4 sts twice. Cast off rem 12 [14] sts.
Collar: With circular needle, cast on 110 sts and work in K1, P1 rib in rounds for 18cm (7in). Cast off loosely in rib.

Making up:
See page 7 for pressing and joining seams. Join seams and sew on collar.

SHORT-SLEEVED SWEATER
Materials:
300 [350]g yarn.

Working instructions:
Back: Work as for long-sleeved sweater until work measures 63cm (24¾in).
Shape neck and shoulders: *next row:* K 25 [30] sts, cast off 40 sts, K to end.
Continue on each group of sts as follows: cast off 5 [6] sts at armhole edge on next and foll 3 [2] alt rows, 7 sts at same edge on foll alt row on large size only; at the same time, cast off 2 sts at neck edge on foll 2 alt rows, then dec 1 st at same edge on foll alt row.
Front: Work as for back until work measures 56cm (22in).
Shape neck: *next row:* K 39 [44] sts, cast off 12, K to end.
Continue on each group of sts, casting off 2 sts at neck edge on every alt row 5 times, then dec 1 st at same edge on every alt row 7 times, then on every 4th row twice. Shape shoulder as for back.
Sleeves: With No 2½mm needles, cast on 82 [88] sts and work in K1, P1 rib for 4cm (1½in).
Change to No 3mm needles and work in st st, inc 1 st at each end of every 4th row 7 times = 96 [102] sts. Continue straight until work measures 12cm (4¾in). Shape top of sleeve as for long-sleeved sweater.
Collar: With circular needle, cast on 140 sts and work in rounds as follows: work alternately 4 rounds K and 4 rounds P at front of work. When work measures 20cm (8in), cast off.

Making up:
As for long-sleeved sweater.

SLEEVELESS SWEATER
Materials:
250 [300]g yarn.

Working instructions:
Back: Work as for short-sleeved sweater.
Front: Work as for back of short-sleeved sweater until work measures 53cm (21in).
Shape neck: *next row:* K 38 [43], cast off 14 sts, K to end.
Continue on each group of sts casting off 2 sts at neck edge on every alt row 4 times, then dec 1 st at same edge on every alt row 6 times, then on every 4th row 1 st 4 times. Continue until work measures 63cm (24¾in), then shape shoulder as on back.
Collar: With circular needle, cast on 180 sts and work in rounds of K2, P2 rib until work measures 20cm (8in). Cast off loosely in rib.
Armhole edging: With circular needle, cast on 140 sts and work in K1, P1 rib for 4cm (1½in). Cast off.

Making up:
As for long-sleeved sweater. Sew armhole edging in place.

The Aran look

The jacket, sweater and cap are knitted in traditional stitches, with diamond panels and cable twists running from waist to neck. The jacket has a snug collar; the sweater has a wide round neck.

BOTH GARMENTS
Sizes:
To fit bust 76–81cm and 86–91cm (30–32in and 34–36in).
Figures in square brackets [ ] refer to second size.

Materials:
Standard double knitting yarn. 1 pair each knitting needles Nos 4 and 5mm (UK sizes 8 and 6); 1 set of knitting needles No 4mm (UK size 8) pointed at both ends; 2 cable needles.

Tension:
21 sts and 26 rows = 10cm (4in).

Aran stitch:
See pattern chart. On wrong-side rows, all P sts of previous row are knitted and all K sts of previous row are purled.
For cable twist, rep 2nd–17th rows, for diamond panel rep 2nd–23rd rows.
Cable 2K and 1P to left: slip 2 sts on a cable needle in front of work, P1, K 2 sts from cable needle.
Cable 1P and 2K to right: slip 1 st on cable needle behind work, K2, then P st from cable needle.
Cable 6 to right: slip 3 sts on a cable needle behind work, K3, then K 3 sts from cable needle.
Cable 6 to left: slip 3 sts on a cable needle in front of work, K3, then K 3 sts from cable needle.
Cable 5 to right: slip 2K and 1P st on cable needle behind the work, K2, slip P st from cable needle back on left-hand needle, place 2 K sts on cable needle in front of work. P st on left-hand needle, K 2 sts from cable needle. When repeating to match in the opposite direction, i.e. cable 5 to *left:* slip 2 sts on cable needle in front of work, slip P st on a cable needle at back of work, K2, P st from cable needle, then K 2 sts from cable needle.

Diamond moss stitch:
1st row (right side): *K1, P1, rep from *.
2nd and 4th rows (wrong side): K the P sts and P the K sts from previous row.
3rd row: *P1, K1, rep from *. Rep rows 1–4.
NB: In K1, P1 rib for welt, K first and last st on every row.

JACKET
Materials:
600g yarn. 1 open-ended zip fastener 60cm (24in) long.

Working instructions:
Back: With No 4mm needles, cast on 97 [105] sts and work in K1, P1 rib, beg after first st with a P st, for 12cm (4¾in).
Change to No 5mm needles and place sts of next row (a wrong-side row) as follows: K1, work 12 sts in K1, P1 rib, K2, work 29 sts as shown on chart, K2, *work 5 [13] sts in

K1, P1 rib = centre of back, then work sts from * in reverse to match first side of back.
On foll rows, work 9 sts in diamond moss st at beg and end of row after first st and before last st. Work straight, working patt from chart until work measures 35cm (13¾in).
Shape armholes by casting off 3 sts at beg of next 2 rows, 2 sts at beg of foll 4 rows, then dec 1 st at each end of every alt row 4 times = 75 [83] sts. Work straight until work measures 53 [54]cm, 20¾ [21¼]in.
Shape neck and shoulders: *next row:* patt 26 [30], cast off 23, patt to end.
Continue on each group of sts by casting off 7 [8] sts at armhole edge on next and foll alt row; at the same time cast off at neck edge on foll alt rows 3 sts once, 2 sts once. Cast off rem 7 [9] sts.
Right front: With No 4mm needles, cast on 50 [54] sts and work in K1, P1 rib, beg after first st with a P st, for 12cm (4¾in).
Change to No 5mm needles and place sts of wrong-side row from side seam as for back up to *, then work 3 [7] sts in K1, P1 rib, then work last st.
Work armhole as for back and continue straight at front edge until work measures 47 [48]cm, 18½ [18¾]in.
Shape neck by casting off at front edge on every alt row as follows: 6 sts once, 3 sts once, 2 sts 3 times, then dec 1 st at same edge on every alt row 3 times. Shape shoulders as for back.
Left front: Work to match right front, reversing shapings.
Sleeves: With No 4mm needles, cast on 42 [46] sts and work 8cm (3¼in) in K1, P1 rib.
Change to No 5mm needles and work in K2, P2 rib. Inc 1 st at each end of every 6th and 8th rows alt 12 times = 66 [70] sts. Continue until work measures 45cm (17¾in).

Shape top of sleeves by casting off at beg of every row as follows: 4 [5] sts twice, 3 sts twice, 2 sts 4 times, then dec 1 st at each end of every alt row once, every 4th row 3 times, every alt row once. Now cast off at beg of every row 2 sts 4 times, 3 sts twice, 4 [5] sts twice. Cast off rem 12 sts.

Making up:
See page 7 for pressing and joining seams. Join seams. With No 4mm needles, pick up 81 sts round neck and work for 26cm (10¼in) in K1, P1 rib. Cast off loosely in rib. Sew zip fastener into place, turning over half of collar outwards and sewing in zip between the 2 halves.

CAP
Materials:
200g yarn.

Working instructions:
Using set of needles pointed at both ends, cast on 108 sts. Work straight for 20cm (8in) in K1, P1 rib.
Place sts as follows: *starting with a P st work 21 sts in K1, P1 rib, 6 sts cable twist as given from 2nd row after the diamond patt on chart, rep 3 times from *.
Continue in Aran stitch for 13cm (5in), then dec as follows: *P1, K2 tog, work 15 sts in rib, K2 tog, P1, 6 st cable twist, rep from * 3 times=100 sts. Rep this dec on every alt round 5 times more, then on every round twice=44 sts.
On every foll round first K tog the 3 centre sts of rib, then P tog the 3 sts between cable twists, then K tog first and last 2 sts of cable twists=20 sts.
Break yarn, thread through remaining sts and fasten off securely.

SWEATER
Materials:
800 [900]g yarn. Needles as for jacket plus 1 circular twin-pin needle No 4mm (UK size 8), 40cm (16in) long.

Working instructions:
Back: With No 4mm needles, cast on 105 [113] sts and work in K1, P1 rib, beg after first st with a P st, until work measures 4cm (1½in).
Change to No 5mm needles and place sts on first wrong-side row as for back of jacket, but at beg and end of the row excluding first and last sts, work 16 sts in rib, working 13 of these sts in diamond moss st on foll right-side row.
When work measures 6cm (2½in), dec 1 st at each end of next row, then dec 1 st at each end of 16th row 3 times=97 [105] sts. Work straight until work measures 45cm (17¾in). Shape armholes as for back of jacket=75 [83] sts. Work straight until work measures 62 [63]cm, 24½ [25]in.
Shape neck and shoulders: next row: patt 22 [26], cast off 31, patt to end. Continue on each group of sts by casting off 2 sts at neck edge on foll 2 alt rows, then dec 1 st at same edge on foll alt row; at the same time cast off at armhole edge on next and foll alt rows 5 sts once, 6 sts once [7 sts twice]. Cast off rem 6 [7] sts.
Front: Work as for back until work measures 55 [56]cm, 21½ [22]in.

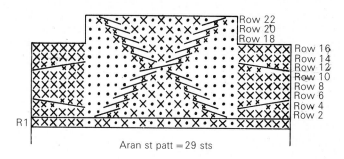

Aran st patt = 29 sts

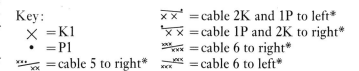

Key:
× = K1
• = P1
= cable 5 to right*

= cable 2K and 1P to left*
= cable 1P and 2K to right*
= cable 6 to right*
= cable 6 to left*

Shape neck: next row: patt 29 [33], cast off 17, patt to end. Continue on each group of sts by casting off at neck edge on every alt row as follows: 3 sts once, 2 sts twice, then dec 1 st at same edge on every alt row 3 times, every 4th row twice. Shape shoulders as for back.
Sleeves: Work as for jacket.

Making up:
See jacket. Using the circular needle, pick up 100 sts round neck, work for 4cm (1½in) in K1, P1 rib. Cast off loosely in rib.

Freewheeling

A maxi-sweater with plenty of freedom for movement. You could easily wear another sweater under it; deep sleeves and yoke are worked in one. Sleeves have elastic threaded cuffs and hemline is picot edged.

Sizes:
76–81cm and 86–91cm (30–32in and 34–36in).
Figures in square brackets [ ] refer to second size.

Materials:
900 [1000]g double knitting yarn, used double throughout. 1 pair knitting needles No 5mm (UK size 6); 1 circular twin-pin needle No 5mm (UK size 6), 40cm (16in) long.

Tension:
14 sts and 20 rows=10cm (4in).

Working instructions:
Back and front (worked alike): Cast on 68 [74] sts and work straight in st st, but after working 3cm (1in), ending with a P row, work holes on next row as follows: K1, *K2 tog, yf, rep from * to last st, K1. On next row P all sts.
When work measures 29cm (11½in), inc 1 st at each end of next row, then inc 1 st at each end of every 4th row 3 times. When work measures 36cm (14in), cast off all 76 [82] sts.
Back and front yoke with sleeves: Starting at left sleeve, cast on 56 [60] sts and work straight in st st, but after working 3cm (1in), work holes on 1 row as described for back and front.
When work measures 25cm (10in), inc as follows: 1 st at each end of next row, 1 st at each end of every 10th row 3 times, 1 st at each end of every 4th and 2nd rows alt 6 times, 1 st at each end of every alt row 10 times and finally cast off 2 sts at beg of next 4 rows=104 [108] sts. Work straight until work measures 73 [75]cm, 28¾ [29½]in.
Divide for neck by working across each group of 52 [54] sts as follows: work right-hand half (back yoke) by dec 1 st at neck edge on next row, then dec 1 st at same edge on every 6th row 3 times=48 [50] sts. Work straight for 12cm (4¾in). Inc 1 st at neck edge of next row, then inc 1 st at neck edge of every 6th row 3 times=52 [54] sts. Leave these stitches on a holder and work front yoke to match.
Work across all 104 [108] sts and complete piece to match, reversing shaping, i.e. dec instead of inc.
Finally pick up 84 sts from neck with the circular needle and work in st st in rounds. When work measures 3cm (1in), work holes on next round as described for back and front. When work measures 6cm (2¼in), cast off.

Making up:
Stitch straight edges of yoke pieces to back and front: see page 9 for pressing and joining seams. Join sleeve seams. Turn under all hems with holes worked in them. Thread elastic through ends of sleeves.

Classic simplicity

A classic pullover with a V-neck which will never go out of fashion. It looks good over a sporty shirt and goes well with trousers and casual skirts. It is shown here in sunny yellow, but knit several in a variety of colours as essentials in your wardrobe.

Sizes:
To fit bust 81–86cm and 91–97cm (34–36 and 37–38in).
Figures in square brackets [ ] refer to second size.

Materials:
300g standard 4 ply yarn. 1 pair each knitting needles Nos 2mm and $2\frac{1}{2}$mm (UK sizes 14 and 12); 1 twin-pin needle No 2mm (UK size 14), 40cm long.

Tension:
27 sts and 38 rows = 10cm (4in).

Working instructions:
Back: With No 2mm needles, cast on 130 [140] sts and work 6cm ($2\frac{1}{4}$in) in K2, P2 rib.
Change to No $2\frac{1}{2}$ needles and work straight in reverse st st until work measures 37cm ($14\frac{1}{2}$in).
Shape armholes by casting off at beg of every row as follows: 4 sts twice, 2 sts 6 times, then dec 1 st at each end of every alt row 4 times = 102 [112] sts. Continue working straight until work measures 50 [51]cm, $19\frac{1}{2}$[20]in.
Shape shoulders by casting off at beg of every row as follows: 5 sts twice [12 times], 4 sts 16 times [6 times], cast off rem 28 sts for neck.
Front: Work as for back until work measures 36cm (14in). Shaping armhole as on back, at the same time shape neck: *next row:* cast off 4 sts, work 61 [66] sts including st on needle after cast off, turn. Now dec at neck edge as follows: 1 st on next row, then on every alt row 11 times; 1 st every 4th row 7 times; 1 st every 6th row 3 times; at the same time, when work measures 50 [51]cm, $19\frac{1}{2}$ [20]in, shape shoulder as for back, omitting last 2 sets of 4 cast-off sts.
Right sleeve: With No 2mm needles, cast on 58 [64] sts and work 6cm ($2\frac{1}{4}$in) in K2, P2 rib.
Continue working in reverse st st, inc 1 st at each end of every 8th row 16 times = 90 [96] sts. Continue straight until work measures 42cm ($16\frac{1}{2}$in).
Shape top of sleeve by casting off at beg of every row as follows: 3 [4] sts 4 times, 2 sts 4 times, then dec 1 st at each end of every alt row 15 times.
Now cast off at beg of every row 2 sts 6 [4] times, 3 sts 4 [6] times. Continue working on rem 16 sts straight for another 12 [14] cm, $4\frac{3}{4}$ [$5\frac{1}{2}$] in, then cast off from right-hand edge on every alt row 4 sts twice, 2 sts 4 times.
Left sleeve: Work to match right sleeve.

Making up:
See page 7 for pressing and joining seams. Join seams. Using the twin-pin needle, pick up 192 sts round the neck and work 1 round K, 1 round P. Continue in K2, P2 rib,

dividing sts so that 2 K sts lie in V of neck, and work 12 rounds, working K2 tog twice on middle 4 sts. Cast off loosely.

Fashion wraparound

You can wrap yourself up in this jacket as if it were a blanket. It is knitted in double knitting yarn – plain or textured – in subtle toning shades, and belted at the waist. Match it with your existing wardrobe to look either casual or elegant.

Sizes:
86–91cm and 97–102cm (34–36in and 38–40in).
Figures in square brackets [ ] refer to second size.

Materials:
Bouclé-type double knitting yarn 240 [280]g in blue, 200 [240]g in dark green, 120 [160]g each in light green and lilac. 1 pair of knitting needles No 4mm (UK size 8); 1 circular twin-pin needle No 4mm (UK size 8), 80cm (32in) long.

Stripe sequence:
*6 rows each in blue, lilac, blue, dark green, light green, dark green, rep from *.

Tension:
15 sts and 26 rows = 10cm (4in).

Working instructions:
The jacket is worked in one piece, beginning at left sleeve. Cast on 78 sts in blue, and work 5 [7] rows in garter st; then work 6 [8] rows each in lilac, blue, dark green and light green in reverse st st.
Continue in reverse st st working 6 rows dark green, then work as shown in stripe sequence until work measures 19cm (7½in). Inc 1 st at each end of next and foll 3 alt rows, then cast on 2 sts at beg of every row 6 times. Now cast on 63 sts at beg of next 2 rows = 224 sts.
Change to circular needle and working straight, work stripe sequence, working 5 sts at each end in garter st and all other sts in reverse st st until work measures 42 [44]cm, 16½ [17½]in. Work 5 sts in garter st at right-hand side of work, then 98 sts in reverse st st, work rem 98 sts in garter st for left front edge, 6 rows each in blue, lilac and blue.
In last row of blue on wrong side of work, cast off 116 sts at left-hand edge, then work the 3 green stripes on rem 108 sts at centre back of work, working 5 sts each end in garter st.
Finally cast on 116 sts in blue for right front, and work other half of jacket to match, reversing shapings.

Making up:
See page 7 for pressing and joining seams. Join side and sleeve seams, sewing bottom 11cm (4½in) of sleeve seam on right side, for turn-up of cuff. *For belt:* cast on 210 [220] sts in dark green, work 6 rows each of dark green and light green in garter st, cast off.

Sporting successes

Great outdoor looks for men. Two sweaters in exciting textures in chunky-type yarns. One is knitted in a ribbed pattern and the other one is worked in a pattern giving an unusual woven effect.

BOTH GARMENTS
Sizes:
To fit chest 97–102cm and 107–112cm (38–40in and 42–44in).
Figures in square brackets [ ] refer to second size.

Materials:
1000 [1100]g double double knitting yarn; 1 pair knitting needles No 6mm (UK size 4); 1 40cm (16in) No 6mm (UK size 4) circular twin-pin needle.

Tension:
14 sts and 20 rows = 10cm (4in).

RUST-COLOURED SWEATER
Stitch pattern:
Worked in multiples of 10 + 2.
1st row (right side): K1, *K2 (P2 and K2) twice, P10, rep from * to last st, K1.
2nd row (and all foll wrong-side rows): K all P sts and P all K sts from previous row.
3rd row: K1, *K2 (P2 and K2) twice, K10, rep from * to last st, K1. *5th row*: as 1st row.
7th row: as 3rd row.
9th row: as 1st row.
Rows 11–20: as rows 1 to 10 but staggering the patt by starting with P10 after working 1st st, i.e. *11th row*: K1, *P10, K2, (P2 and K2) twice, rep from * to last st, K1.

Working instructions:
Back: Cast on 72 [82] sts and work 8cm (3in) in K2, P2 rib. Continue working straight in patt until work measures 68cm (26¾in). *Next row*: patt 25 [28], cast off 22 [26], patt to end. Cast off at neck edge on each group of sts 2 sts once, then dec 1 st at same edge on foll alt row. Cast off rem 22 [25] sts for shoulder.
Front: Work as for back until work measures 60cm (23½in). *Next row*: patt 31 [34], cast off 10 [14], patt to end. Cast off at neck edge on each group of sts 2 sts on every alt row 3 times, then dec 1 st on every alt row 3 times. Cast off rem 22 [25] sts for shoulder.
Sleeves: Cast on 42 sts and work 8cm (3in) in K2, P2 rib. Continue in patt, inc 1 st at each end of every 8th row 10 times [1 st at each end of every 6th and 8th rows alt 12 times] = 62 [66] sts. Continue until work measures 55 [56]cm, 21½ [22]in, cast off.
Neckband: With the circular needle, cast on 80 [84] sts and work 4cm (1½in) in K2, P2 rib.

Making up:
See page 7 for pressing and joining seams. Join seams and sew on neckband.

GREEN SWEATER
Stitch pattern:
Multiples of 6 + 2.
1st row (right side): K1, *K4, P2, rep from * to last st, K1.
2nd row (wrong side): K1, *K3, P3, rep from * to last st, K1.
3rd row: K1, *K2, P4, rep from * to last st, K1.
4th row: K1, *K5, P1, rep from * to last st, K1. Rep 1st to 4th rows.

Working instructions:
Back: Cast on 74 [80] sts, work in K2, P2 rib for 8cm (3in). Continue working straight in patt until work measures 68cm (26¾in). *Next row*: patt 26 [28], cast off 22 [24], patt to end. Cast off at neck edge on each group of sts 2 sts once, then dec 1 st at same edge on foll alt row. Cast off rem 23 [25] sts for shoulder.
Front: Work as back until work measures 45cm (17¾in). *Next row*: patt 37 [40], turn. Dec 1 st at neck edge on every alt row 8 times, then dec 1 st at neck edge of every 4th row 6 [7] times. Cast off rem 23 [25] sts for shoulder.

Sleeves: Cast on 38 sts and work 8cm (3in) in K2, P2 rib. Continue working in patt, inc 1 st at each end of every 6th and 8th rows alt 12 times [1 st at each end of every 6th row 14 times]=62 [66] sts. When work measures 55 [56]cm, 21½ [22]in, cast off.

Neckband: With the circular needle, cast on 123 [127] sts and work in rounds in K2, P2 rib, starting with K3 for centre front and at each dec knitting 3 sts tog at this point (i.e. 1 st lying each side of central st plus central st). Dec as follows: *1 round without dec, dec on next 2 rounds, rep from *. Work 6cm (2½in) in this way.

Making up:
As for rust-coloured sweater.

Sunshine set

Perfect for packing when you go on holiday: a summer twin set with all sorts of possibilities. The sleeveless jacket also would go well with blouses or polo-neck sweaters. It is crocheted with a mohair-type yarn, with knitted edgings in the same wool as the halter top, which is knitted throughout.

BOTH GARMENTS
Sizes:
To fit bust 81–86cm and 91–97cm (32–34in and 36–38in). Figures in square brackets [ ] refer to second size.

HALTER TOP
Materials:
200 [250]g standard 4 ply yarn in plain green. 1 circular twin-pin needle No $2\frac{1}{2}$mm (UK size 12); 1 pair of No $2\frac{1}{2}$mm (UK size 12) knitting needles. Elastic.

Tension (measured without stretching):
36 sts and 36 rounds (use rows for tension sample)=10cm (4in).

Working instructions:
Back and front: Worked in rounds in one piece. Using the circular twin-pin needle, for a width of 68 [72]cm, $26\frac{3}{4}$ [$28\frac{1}{4}$]in, cast on 246 [260] sts and work in K1, P1 rib for 45cm ($17\frac{3}{4}$in). Cast off loosely in rib.
Halter: Cast on 15 sts and work in K1, P1 rib, slipping first st of every row for 60cm ($23\frac{1}{2}$in).

Making up:
Turn top edge 4cm ($1\frac{1}{2}$in) over on the outside, inserting elastic into fold and holding in place with herringbone-st casing. Sew ends of halter into place 16cm ($6\frac{1}{4}$in) apart.

SLEEVELESS JACKET
Materials:
280 [320]g mohair-type 4 ply yarn in random green shade, 100g standard 4 ply yarn in plain green. 1 No 4.50mm (UK size 7) crochet hook; 1 circular twin-pin needle No $2\frac{1}{2}$mm (UK size 12), 120cm (48in) long. Lining for pockets.

Tension:
25 sts=5 stitch clusters and 10 rows=10cm (4in).

Pattern:
Foundation chain in multiples of 3+1.
1st row (wrong side): 1 tr into 4th ch from hook, 2 ch, 1 dc, *miss 2 sts, into next st work 2 tr, 2 ch, 1 dc, rep from * to end.
2nd row (right side): 2 turning ch, *into ch space of previous row work 2 tr, 2 ch, 1 dc, rep from * to end. Rep 2nd row.
Edging: K1, P1 rib.

Working instructions:
Back: Make 79 [85] foundation ch and work straight in patt=26 [28] clusters=130 [140] sts. When work measures 8cm ($3\frac{1}{4}$in) inc 1 st at each end of next and every 10th row

4 times=120 [130] sts. Continue until work measures 51cm (20in).
Shape armholes by dec 5 sts at each end of every row twice= 100 [110] sts. Work straight until work measures 71 [72]cm, 28 [$28\frac{1}{2}$]in.
Leaving centre 36 [42] sts unworked, continue on each group of sts, dec at neck edge on every row as follows: 2 sts once, 1 st twice; at the same time, when work measures 72 [73]cm, $28\frac{1}{2}$ [$28\frac{3}{4}$]in, dec 14 [15] sts on every row twice for shoulders.
Left front: Make 24 [37] ch and work in patt=11 [12] clusters=55 [60] sts.
Work side seam, armhole and shoulder as for back. When work measures 18cm (7in), work pocket as follows: next row: work 5 sts from front edge, then make 27 ch; miss foll 45 sts, work to end.
Continue in patt, working straight at front edge until work measures 45cm ($17\frac{3}{4}$in). Shape front edge by dec 1 st on next and every alt row 11 [14] times.
Right front: Work to match left front.
Edging: Using circular twin-pin needle and plain wool, cast on 577 [585] sts and work in rows in rib for 4cm ($1\frac{1}{2}$in); cast off loosely in rib.
Armhole edging: Using plain wool, cast on 144 [148] sts and work in rib for 4cm ($1\frac{1}{2}$in).
Pocket edging: Using plain wool, cast on 60 sts, work in rib for 4cm ($1\frac{1}{2}$in); cast off loosely in rib.

Making up:
See page 7 for pressing and joining seams. Cut pockets and sew in place. Join seams. Sew edgings to cast-on edges. Turn lower edge 4cm ($1\frac{1}{2}$in) under and stitch in place.

Pretty as a picture

These tank tops are worked in stocking stitch and garter stitch with oddments of yarn. One has a truck on the front and the other a house. The backs are worked in colours to match up with the background colours of the bands on the fronts.

BOTH TANK TOPS
Size:
To fit chest 56cm (22in).

Materials:
Quantities of double knitting yarn in the colours given for each design. 1 pair each knitting needles Nos 3½mm and 4mm (UK sizes 9 and 8).

Tension over stocking stitch:
20 sts and 30 rows = 10cm (4in).

Tension over garter stitch:
20 sts and 40 rows = 10cm (4in).

BOY'S TANK TOP
Materials:
Standard double knitting yarn: approximately 50g each grey and olive green and 25g each dark green, blue, red, black, white and natural.

Working instructions:
Back (worked in stripes): With No 3½mm needles, cast on 56 sts in olive, and work in K1, P1 rib for 4cm (1¾in).
Change to No 4mm needles and work in st st 4 rows olive, then 36 rows grey.
Change to garter st and work 14 rows olive, then continue in blue; at the same time, after 6 rows have been worked in olive, shape armholes as follows: cast off 3 sts at beg of next 2 rows, 2 sts at beg of foll 2 rows, then dec 1 st at each end of foll 3 alt rows = 40 sts.
Continue until work measures 13cm (5in) from start of garter st. *Next row:* K8, cast off 24, K to end.
Continue working straight on each group of 8 sts until work measures 15cm (6in) from start of garter st. Cast off 4 sts at armhole edge on next and foll alt row.
Front: Work welt as for back.
Change to st st and work 4 rows in olive, 4 rows in grey, then using separate balls of yarn, work from chart, keeping 8 sts in grey on either side of chart and working armhole shaping as for back.
Continue working until design from chart has been completed, then K 6 rows and shape neck and complete shoulders as for back.

Making up:
See page 7 for pressing and joining seams. Join seams.

GIRL'S TANK TOP
Materials:
Approximately 50g in emerald and blue and 25g each in white, grey, black, red and light blue.

Working instructions:
Work as described for boy's top, working 4cm (1¾in) emerald garter st instead of olive ribbing. For *back* work 36 rows in emerald st st, and finally change to blue garter st to finish.
On *front* follow chart of house instead of truck design, keeping 8 sts either side in emerald. Follow picture for colours, and work in st st, noting that the V sts are in blue and slipped over 2 rows.

Key to boy's chart:

X = 1 K st at front of work
O = 1 P st at front of work

Chart shows centre 40 sts of front. After 36 rows, only right-side rows are shown. K sts on wrong-side rows in the same colours as on previous row.

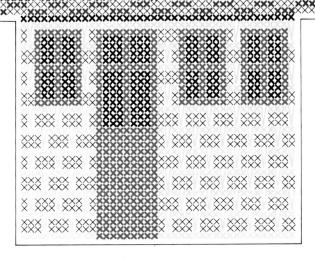

Key to girl's chart:

X = 1 K st at front of work.
V = slip st over 2 rows.

Cool cream

Natural-coloured cotton or synthetic yarn, such as courtelle, is best for both these models. Her sweater is knitted in garter stitch, all in one piece. His has a chunky ribbed pattern, and sleeves set in straight. The trimmings in strong cotton fabric are both smart and practical as they help the sweaters to keep their shape.

BOTH SWEATERS
Materials:
Standard double knitting yarn, preferably cotton or synthetic.

MAN'S SWEATER

Sizes:
To fit chest 102–107cm and 111–117cm (40–42in and 44–46in). Figures in square brackets [ ] refer to second size.

Materials:
1000 [1100]g yarn. 1 pair each knitting needles No $3\frac{1}{2}$mm (UK size 9) and $4\frac{1}{2}$mm (UK size 7). 40cm ($15\frac{3}{4}$in) of cotton fabric 91cm (36in) wide. 2 buttons.

Pattern:
Worked in multiples of 4 + 1.
1st row (wrong side): K1, *K3, P1, rep from *; at end of row K4.
2nd row (right side): K2, P1, *K3, P1, rep from * to last 2 sts, K2.
Rep rows 1 and 2.

Tension:
16 sts and 22 rows = 10cm (4in).

Working instructions:
Back and front: With No $3\frac{1}{2}$mm needles, cast on 81 [85] sts and work straight in patt until work measures 8cm ($3\frac{1}{4}$in).
Change to No $4\frac{1}{2}$mm needles and continue until work measures 70cm ($27\frac{1}{2}$in). *Next row:* patt 26 [28], cast off 29, patt to end. Leave the 26 [28] sts at each side of cast-off sts on spare needles for shoulders.
Sleeves: With No $3\frac{1}{2}$mm needles, cast on 49 sts and work straight in patt until work measures 5cm (2in).
Change to No $4\frac{1}{2}$mm needles and continue working in patt, inc 1 st at each end of next row, then inc 1 st at each end of every 4th and 6th row alternately 17 times = 85 sts. Continue in patt until work measures 48cm (19in). Cast off.

Making up:
Knit shoulder seams of back and front tog on wrong side by knitting 1 st from each needle tog each time; at the same time cast off.
Cut out 2 shoulder patches and 2 elbow patches with 1cm (just under $\frac{1}{2}$in) seam allowance. Turn under and press seam allowances. Cut shoulder tabs 4 times with 1cm (just under $\frac{1}{2}$in) seam allowance; sew 2 sets of shoulder tabs tog and turn right side out.
For sleeve binding: cut 2 strips 32cm ($12\frac{1}{2}$in) long and 6cm ($2\frac{1}{4}$in) wide and bind ends of sleeves.
Baste elbow patches into place 8cm (3in) from top of sleeve, positioning them in centre of sleeve piece; stitch through twice, once close to the edge, once about 1cm (just under $\frac{1}{2}$in) in from edge.
Sew sleeves to back and front, centre of sleeve matching shoulder seam. Place shoulder patches in position with centre of patch to seam of sleeves and baste; place shoulder tab on back of patch, laying it along shoulder seam, baste narrow side to seam of sleeve and shoulder. Stitch shoulder patches in place in the same way as elbow patches, stitching in shoulder tab at the same time. Sew buttons to shoulder tabs. Join all remaining seams of work, threading elastic through binding round sleeves if desired.

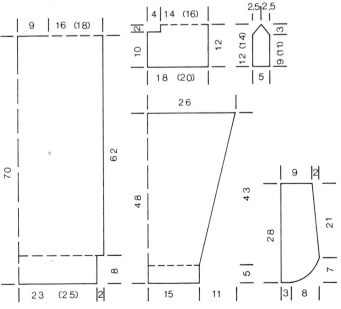

Pattern pieces (not full size; measurements are in centimetres): $\frac{1}{2}$ back and front (worked the same), $\frac{1}{2}$ sleeve, 1 left shoulder patch, 1 shoulder tab and left elbow patch.

WOMAN'S SWEATER

Sizes:
To fit bust 81–86cm and 91–97cm (32–34in and 36–38in). Figures in square brackets [ ] refer to second size.

Materials:
1000 [1100]g yarn. 1 pair knitting needles No 4½mm (UK size 7). 60cm (24in) of cotton fabric 91cm (36in) wide. 10 buttons.

Pattern:
Garter st = K every row.

Tension:
15 sts and 20 rows = 10cm (4in).

Working instructions:
Sweater is worked sideways in one piece. Starting with left sleeve, cast on 60 [64] sts and work straight in patt until work measures 30cm (12in). Now inc 1 st at each end of next and foll 7 alt rows, then cast on 50 sts more at beg of next 2 rows for side seam = 176 [180] sts. Work straight until work measures 40 [41]cm, 15½ [16]in.

Divide work in centre for shoulder slit, working back first as follows: work across 88 [90] sts, turn and work straight for 10 [11]cm, 4 [4½]in along edge of shoulder slit, then cast off 3 sts at neck edge = 85 [87] sts. Work straight for 20cm (8in) then cast on 3 sts at neck edge. Work another 10 [11]cm, 4 [4½]in on these 88 [90] sts; then leave them on a spare needle.

Now work on sts for front as follows: work straight for 10 [11]cm, 4 [4½]in along edge of shoulder slit; at the same time, after 5cm (2in) have been worked, cast off 24 sts at lower edge of work for pocket slit; cast on 24 sts on next row. Work now measures 50 [52]cm, 19½ [20½]in.

Cast off 12 sts at neck edge = 76 [78] sts; work 20cm (8in) straight, then cast on 12 sts at neck edge = 88 [90] sts. At edge of shoulder slit, work another 10 [11]cm, 4 [4½]in; at the same time, after 5 [6]cm, 2 [2¼]in have been worked, work 2nd pocket slit as 1st. Now work across both sets of 88 [90] sts = 176 [180] sts and complete pullover to match beg of work.

Making up:

Cut out fabric pieces as follows: for the loops, cut a strip 76cm (30in) long and 3cm (1in) wide, sew tog to make a tube, turn right side out and press. Cut into 10 pieces each 7cm (3in) long, and halfway along form to a point; stitch down the point. Cut bindings for back and front with triangular pieces according to patt, leaving 1cm (just under $\frac{1}{2}$in) seam allowance; baste into position, inserting 3 loops in place on both front shoulder bindings. Stitch all pieces close to the edge.

For pocket trimmings, cut 4 strips 7cm (3in) wide and 17cm (6$\frac{1}{2}$in) long, and 2 triangles as for binding at neck. For pocket lining, cut 1 piece 17cm (6$\frac{1}{2}$in) wide and 32 [33]cm, 12$\frac{1}{2}$ [13]in long. Turn in and press long sides of strips and seam allowances of triangles. Baste strips close to pocket slit, basting triangles in place above; stitch close to the edges. Trim pocket lining and sew in by hand.

For binding round bottom of sweater, cut 2 strips, 16cm (6$\frac{1}{4}$in) wide and 48cm (19in) long, turn in and press seam allowance. Fold strips in half and bind lower edges of garment, easing knitting in place gently, and stitching 2 loops in place at each short side of front binding. Stitch through bindings close to edge.

For sleeve bindings, cut 2 strips 42 [43]cm, 16$\frac{1}{2}$ [17]in long and 6cm (2$\frac{1}{4}$in) wide; bind edges of sleeves. Finally join side and sleeve seams, leaving 10cm (4in) open at bottom of side seams. Sew on buttons.

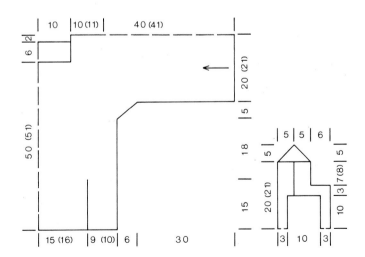

Pattern pieces (not full size; measurements are in centimetres): $\frac{1}{2}$ back and front, $\frac{1}{2}$ sleeve, $\frac{1}{2}$ back and front bindings.

Fashion crochet
Follow the trend

This long crochet waistcoat in a lively shade of double knit yarn is a very simple shape. Edges are worked in double crochet.

It looks stunning in a tweedy mix for country wear, or ring the changes in other colours for a more dressy version. Deep pockets add the essential fashion touch.

Sizes:
To fit bust 86–91cm and 97–102 cm (34–36in and 38–40in).
Figures in square brackets [ ] refer to second size.

Materials:
700 [750]g tweed-look double knitting yarn. 1 crochet hook No 5.00mm (UK size 6).

Tension:
18 sts and 11 rows = 10cm (4in).

Stitch pattern:
Foundation chain worked in multiples of 4 + 1.
1st row: 1 turning ch, 1 dc in 2nd st from hook, *1 ch, miss 1 st, dc in next st, rep from *.
2nd row: 3 ch for turning chain, *1 tr into 2nd foll ch sp, 1 ch, 1 tr round missed ch of previous row, 1 tr into next dc, rep from *.
3rd row: 1 turning ch, 1 dc into 1st tr, *1ch, 1dc into ch sp between crossed trs, 1 ch, 1 dc into uncrossed tr, rep from *; at end of row, work last dc into top of turning ch. Rep 2nd and 3rd rows.

Working instructions:
Back: Make 101 [109] ch + 1 turning ch. Work in patt, dec 1 st at each end of every 4th row 8 times = 85 [93] sts.
Continue working straight until work measures 42cm (16½in). Shape armholes by dec 2 sts at each end of next 3 rows, 1 st at each end of next 4 rows, 1 st at each end of every alt row twice = 61 [69] sts.
Continue working straight until work measures 68 [69]cm, 26¾ [27] in.
Leaving centre 23 [27] sts unworked for back of neck, shape shoulders and neck on each group of sts by dec 8 [9] sts at armhole edge and 2 sts at neck edge on next row, 8 [9] sts at armhole edge and 1 st at neck edge on foll row. Fasten off.
Left front: Make 49 [50] ch + 1 turning ch and work in patt shaping side seam, armhole and shoulder to match back and shaping front slope as follows: when work measures 30cm (12in), dec 1 st at front edge on next row, then dec 1 st 12 [14] more times at same edge on every 3rd row. Fasten off.
Right front: Work to match left front.
Pockets: For pockets 18cm (7in) wide make 33 + 1 ch and work for 20cm (8in) in patt. Work 2 rows double crochet at top edge.

Making up:
See page 7 for pressing and joining seams. Join seams. Work 2 rows double crochet round edges, working 45 sts along straight edges of fronts, 60 [64] sts along front neck shapings, 25 [27] sts along back of neck. Sew on pockets.

Summer chic

A useful, cool jacket in crochet which can be worn without a blouse in summer. On chillier days, wear it as a shortie cardigan for that extra touch of warmth. It is such a useful style to mix and match with dresses and separates for your holiday wardrobe.

Sizes:
To fit bust 86–91cm and 97–102cm (34–36in and 38–40 in). Figures in square brackets [ ] refer to second size.

Materials:
350 [400]g standard 4 ply yarn. 1 No 3mm (UK size 11) crochet hook.

Tension:
26 sts and 13 rows = 10cm (4in).

Pattern for welt and edging:
Double crochet. Begin each row with 1 turning ch, work dc into every st to end.

Main pattern:
1st row (wrong-side): work in tr, starting in 3rd st from hook.
2nd row (right side): make 3 turning ch, *1 ch, miss 1 st, 1 tr into next st, rep from * to end of row.
3rd row: 2 turning ch, 1 tr into each tr and each ch space. Rep 2nd and 3rd rows.

Working instructions:
Back: Beg at right side seam, make 79 ch + 2 turning ch, work in patt, working straight at left-hand side for bottom edge, while inc at right-hand side for armhole as follows: inc 1 st every 2nd row twice, 1 st every row once, 2 sts every row once [twice], 3 sts every row once, 8 sts every row once, then inc 36 more sts = 131 [133] sts.
Continue inc at right-hand side of work for shoulder as follows: inc 1 st every alt row [every 2nd and 3rd rows alt] 4 times = 135 [137] sts.
When work measures 14 [16]cm, $5\frac{1}{2}$ [$6\frac{1}{4}$]in, dec for neck at right-hand side as follows: dec 2 sts once, then dec 1 st every row twice = 131 [133] sts. Work straight until work measures 24 [26]cm, $9\frac{1}{2}$ [$10\frac{1}{4}$]in; this is centre of work.
Crochet other half of back to match, reversing shapings, i.e. dec instead of inc and vice versa.
Left front: Work as for back until work measures 14 [16]cm, $5\frac{1}{2}$ [$6\frac{1}{4}$]in, then dec for neck at right-hand side as follows: dec 11 sts every row 3 times, 5 sts every row 3 times, 2 sts every row 6 times, work last row over the rem 75 [77] sts. Fasten off.
Right front: Work to match left front.
Sleeves: Make 19 ch + 2 turning ch and work in patt, inc at right-hand edge of work for top of sleeve as follows: inc 1 st every 2nd row twice, then in every row inc 1 st twice, 2 sts 2 [3] times, 3 sts 6 times, 2 sts twice, 1 st twice, then 1 st every 2nd row twice = 53 [55] sts.
Continue working straight until 18 [19]cm, 7 [$7\frac{1}{2}$]in have been worked; this is centre of sleeve. Work other half of sleeve to match.
Cuffs: Make 82 [86] ch + 1 turning ch and work 12cm ($4\frac{3}{4}$in) in dc. Fasten off.
Welt: Make 214 [232] ch + 1 turning ch and work 4cm ($1\frac{1}{2}$in) in dc. Fasten off.
Front edging: Make 308 [314] ch + 1 turning ch and work in dc for 4cm ($1\frac{1}{2}$in), working buttonholes by missing 3 sts and working 3 ch, 2cm ($\frac{3}{4}$in) from edge; work first buttonhole 1.5cm ($\frac{1}{2}$in) from bottom right edge, then 3 more at intervals of 8 [8.5]cm, 3 [$3\frac{1}{2}$]in. Fasten off.

Making up:
See page 7 for pressing and joining seams. Join seams, sew on edgings, sewing 8cm (3in) of cuffs on right side, for turn-up.

Ethnic enchantment

This jacket, with an exotic Mexican look, will make you stand out from the crowd. The contrast of bright stripes on white is very striking; you can vary the colours as you like within the areas given in the plan. The photographs show you the effect. It is loose fitting, comfortable to wear, with voluminous sleeves.

Size:
To fit bust 86–91cm (34–36in).

Materials:
Standard 4 ply yarn. 550g in white, 25g each in 11 assorted colours. 1 crochet hook No 3.50mm (UK size 9).

Pattern:
Half treble, each row beginning in 1st st after 2 turning ch and ending in last st. When changing colour within a row, make last loop of a st in the new colour.

Tension:
18 sts and 14 rows = 10cm (4in).

Working instructions:
The jacket is worked in one piece, working horizontally. Starting with right sleeve, make 94 ch + 2 turning ch in white and work in pattern. Use a strand of contrasting yarn between 2 centre sts to mark centre of sleeve and shoulder. Continue working as shown in plan, working coloured stripes within the areas shown (colours can be of your own choice). When work measures 29cm (11½in) make 49 sts more each side for back and right front. When work measures 55cm (21¾in) leave 141 sts unworked at right, work straight for back of neck. After centre row marked on plan, complete other half of work to match.

Belt: Length 130cm (51¼in). Make 230 ch + 2 turning ch in white, work 5 rows in htr.

Making up:
See page 7 for pressing and joining seams. Join side and sleeve seams. Work 1 row dc round edges, working 3 dc into every 2 rows of pattern.

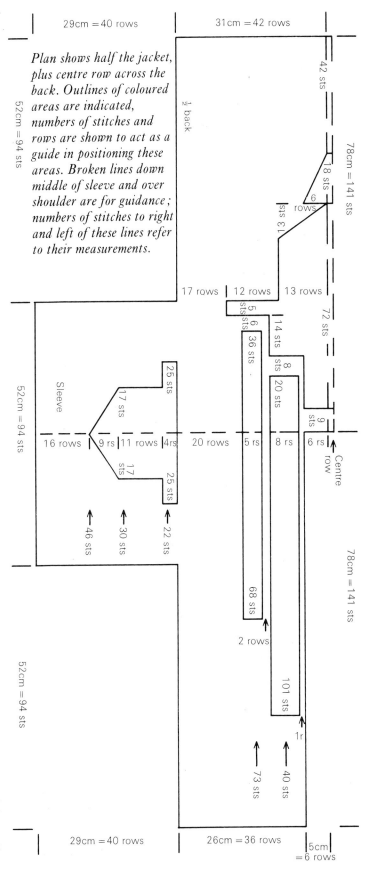

Plan shows half the jacket, plus centre row across the back. Outlines of coloured areas are indicated, numbers of stitches and rows are shown to act as a guide in positioning these areas. Broken lines down middle of sleeve and over shoulder are for guidance; numbers of stitches to right and left of these lines refer to their measurements.

Smart striping

An eye-catching striped design makes this tank top smart as well as sporty and an all-year-round favourite. It can be worn with matching or contrasting shirts and trousers. Main parts on back and front are worked sideways in a variation of treble and the borders are worked in double crochet.

Sizes:
86–91cm and 97–102cm (34–36in and 38–40in).
Figures in square brackets [ ] refer to second size.

Materials:
Standard 4 ply yarn. 150g in white, 50g in black. 1 crochet hook No 3.00mm (UK size 11).

Pattern:
1st row: starting in 3rd ch from hook, work tr patt = yarn round hook, insert hook into stitch, pull loop through, yarn round hook, draw through 1 loop, yarn round hook, draw through 3 rem loops.
2nd row: 2 turning ch, starting in first st work mock tr, inserting hook through both parts of sts on previous row.
3rd row: 1 turning ch, starting in 1st st work dc, inserting hook only through parts of sts on previous row now lying at front of work.
4th row: 1 turning ch, starting in 1st st work dc, inserting hook only through parts of sts on previous row now lying at back of work.
5th row: 2 turning ch, starting in 1st st work mock tr, inserting hook through parts of sts on previous row now lying at front of work. Rep rows 2 to 5.

Stripes:
*2 rows white, 2 rows black, rep from *.

Border pattern:
Starting with a right-side row, work dc, working only into back parts of sts on previous row when working right-side rows, working through both parts of sts on previous row when working wrong-side rows.

Tension:
23 sts and 13 rows = 10cm (4in).

Working instructions:
Back: Starting at right-hand side seam, make 71 [74] ch + 2 turning ch in white and work in patt, foll stripe sequence, keeping work straight at left, i.e. lower, edge. At right side, shape armhole when work measures 2cm ($\frac{3}{4}$in): then inc 1 st on next 5 rows. Now inc 3 sts on every row 3 times = 85 [88] sts. Make 32 [35] more ch = 117 [123] sts: work should measure 8cm (3in) from beg. Shape shoulders by inc 1 st on every 3rd [4th] row 3 times = 120 [126] sts. When work measures 15 [17]cm, 6 [6$\frac{1}{2}$]in, shape neck as follows: dec 2 sts next 2 rows, 1 st on next row = 115 [121] sts. Work straight until work measures 26cm (10$\frac{1}{4}$in) at centre of back. Work other half of back to match, reversing shapings.
Front: Work as for back up to neck shaping. When work measures 15 [17]cm, 6 [6$\frac{1}{2}$]in, dec 16 sts once, 12 sts once, 4 sts on next 3 rows, 3 sts on next 4 rows, 2 sts on next 2 rows, 1 st on next 2 rows = 62 [68] sts; work should measure 24 [26]cm, 10 [10$\frac{3}{4}$]in = centre front. Work other half of front to match, reversing shapings.

Making up:
See page 7 for pressing and joining seams. Join seams. Work 1 row sl st round lower armholes and neck edge, then in white, work borders into this row: first work 2 rounds in black, then continue in white. *Welt:* working in border patt, work 220 [240] sts all round on 1st round. Then continue in patt until welt measures 10cm (4in); fasten off. *Armholes:* 110 [116] sts; after 2 rounds in black, work 5 rounds in white. *Neckband:* starting at centre front work in rows as for armholes; stitch narrow ends of rows together right over left.

Bright crochet caps

You need something to complete your new outfit, but a hat would look too formal . . . little crochet caps in a matching colour, like these, are the perfect solution. Simple to work, you can make several caps in various colours to wear with different outfits.

Size:
Average head size.

Materials:
100g of standard double knitting yarn. 1 crochet hook No 4.00mm (UK size 8).

Tension:
18 sts and 22 rounds = 10cm (4in).

Pattern:
Double crochet; every round beginning with 1 turning ch, then work into 2nd st, every round ending with 1 slip st into 1st double crochet.

Working instructions:
Starting at centre, make a loop in yarn, make 1 ch, make 8 dc into loop, pull loop tog, 1 sl st into 1st dc.
Continue working rounds to and fro in patt, inc as follows:
2nd round (return round): work twice into every st = 16sts.
3rd round (forward round): work twice into every alt st = 24 sts.
4th round: work twice into every 4th st.
5th round: work twice into 1st and every foll 5th st.
6th round: work twice into every 6th st.
7th round: work twice into 1st and every foll 7th st.
8th round: work twice into every 8th st = 54 sts.
Continue inc only on return rounds: in 10th round inc in every 9th st; in 12th round inc in every 10th st; in 14th round inc in every 11th st; in 16th round inc in every 12th st; in 18th round inc in every 13th st; in 20th round inc in every 14th st = 90 sts.
Continue working without further inc until work measures approximately 20cm (7¾in) = 44 rounds. End with a return round because of turned-up brim.
For loop at top, make 10 ch + 1 turning ch, work 2 rows dc; fasten off. Sew loop tog into ring and sew to middle of cap.

Cobweb finery

For festive evenings: a triangular shawl as delicate and sparkling as a cobweb. It is made in hairpin crochet in a pattern of contrasting textures – soft yarn and glittering Lurex.

Size:
55cm (21½in) from upper edge to pointed end (not counting fringe).

Materials:
25g mohair and metal, 20g angora-type yarn, 40g fine Lurex. If you have difficulty in obtaining the speciality yarns used in the original shawl, you can work it successfully in 2 ply yarn; approximately 85g 2 ply; 1 hairpin crochet prong 7cm (3in), 1 crochet hook No 3.00mm (UK size 11).

Width of border:
8cm (3in) = position 1 + 5 on hairpin prong.

Shawl pattern:
First work separate loops in basic hairpin stitch, then crochet together to form clusters down centre back and at corners of shawl (see working pictures 1–5 and close-up of corner clusters).

Basic hairpin stitch:
1 Using crochet hook, make a loop over the right-hand pin of the prong, knot lying in the middle. *Turn prong from right to left, insert hook into left-hand loop from below and work 1 dc. Rep from *.

Clusters:
2 When all loops have been worked for the strips, work the edges. Work twisted clusters at sides and centre along top of strip, taking up the number of loops given in the instructions and twisting them from left to right.
3 Secure cluster by working group of loops on hook together with 1 dc, make 5 ch. Illustration shows hook in position to take up the next 3 loops.
4 Work 5 ch between each set of loops.
5 The lower edge is worked without corners; take up 3 loops as before and join with 1 dc. Work in this way all along the strip, making 5 ch between each set of loops.

Working instructions:
First work strips separately in mohair and metal yarn, then join with angora yarn.
1st strip: Work 114 loops in hairpin crochet pattern. Then, working along one edge (top edge) take up 15 loops for twisted cluster, join with 1 dc, twisting from left to right (picture 2, left). Make 5 ch. Then join 3 loops with 1 dc 9 times in the normal way (pictures 3 and 4, left); make 5 ch. For the corners and centre back: work 30 loops twisted and joined with 1 dc; work alternately 5 ch and 3 loops joined by 1 dc 9 times, then make 5 ch, join 15 loops twisted with 1 dc. In this and all other strips work other edge (lower edge) as follows: *join 3 loops with 1 dc, 5 ch (picture 5, left).

Rep from *. At end, join 3 loops.
2nd strip: Work 162 loops. Using method described for 1st strip, join along top edge 15 loops once, 3 loops 17 times, 30 loops once, 3 loops 17 times, 15 loops once, working 5 ch between each set of loops.
3rd strip: Work 216 loops. Top edge: join 15 loops once, 3 loops 26 times, 30 loops once, 3 loops 26 times, 15 loops once, making 5 ch between each set of loops.
4th strip: Work 264 loops. Top edge: join 15 loops once, 3 loops 34 times, 30 loops once, 3 loops 34 times, 15 loops once, making 5 ch between each set of loops.
Then join strips with Lurex: 1 dc into centre ch of 1st ch arch at top edge of 2nd strip, 3 ch, 1 dc into centre ch of 1st ch arch at lower edge of 1st strip, 3 ch. Continue working in this way until all ch arches are joined. Join other strips in the same way.
Work sides with angora yarn: *dc into dc joining 15 loops, dc round set of 3 loops, dc into centre of strip, dc round set of 3 loops, dc into dc joining 3 loops, dc into dc of row worked in Lurex, making 5 ch between each dc, repeat from *.
Work all round shawl: 1st round, Lurex: *1 dc into centre ch of a ch arch in angora yarn, 7 ch, repeat from *, joining with sl st into dc. 2nd round, angora: *1 dc into 4th ch of a ch arch in Lurex, 5 ch, repeat from *, finish with sl st.

Making up:
Pin out shawl carefully to shape, cover with damp cloth and leave to dry. For the fringe: cut strands of Lurex 40cm (16in) long and knot 5 strands at a time into each chain arch at lower edge of shawl.

Here you can see the central twisted cluster at corners and centre back of shawl and the crochet joins.

Casual contrasts

Both jackets are made to the same pattern, combining crochet with knitting, in elegant toning shades, but in different crochet stitches and with different necklines. Sleeves, saddle shoulders, front bands and welts are knitted.

BOTH GARMENTS:
Sizes:
To fit chest 107–112cm and 117–122cm (42–44in and 46–48in).
Figures in square brackets [ ] refer to second size.

Materials:
Standard double knitting yarn; 1 pair each knitting needles Nos 3½mm and 4mm (UK sizes 9 and 8); 1 crochet hook No 4.00mm (UK size 8).

Crochet tension:
18 sts and 18 rows = 10cm (4in).

GREY JACKET
Materials:
300 [350]g yarn in dark grey, 250 [300]g each in medium grey and light grey; 4 buttons.

Crochet pattern:
Multiples of 8+3 sts.
1st row (wrong side), light grey: 1 turning ch, 1 dc into 2nd st from hook, *1 ch, miss 1 st, 1 dc into next st, repeat from *.
2nd row (right side), medium grey: 2 turning ch, *1 tr *in front* of work into empty st of foundation ch, 1 ch, 1 tr *behind* work into next empty st of foundation ch, 1 ch, repeat from *. At end of row, 1 tr *in front* of work into last empty st of foundation ch, 1 ch, leave loop hanging free.
3rd row (right side), light grey: insert hook into light-grey loop of row lying below, make 4 turning ch, *work twice alt 1 tr *in front* of work into dc of 1st row and 1 ch, then twice alt 1 tr *behind* work into dc of 1st row and 1 ch, repeat from *. At end of row work twice alt 1 tr *in front* of work into dc and 1 ch, then work 1 tr *behind* work into last dc, working tog with grey loop of 2nd row at the same time.
4th row (wrong side), medium grey: as for 2nd row, working tr into grey tr sts.
5th row (wrong side), light grey: as for 3rd row, working tr into light-grey tr sts.
6th row (right side), medium grey: as for 4th row.
7th row (right side), light grey: as for 5th row, but staggering placing of trs, i.e. beginning and ending with 2 tr *behind* work.
8th row (wrong side), medium grey: as for 4th row.
9th row (wrong side), light grey: as for 7th row. Rep rows 2–9.

Working instructions:
Back: Make 99 [107] ch in light grey and work straight in crochet patt until work measures 37cm (14½in). Shape armholes by dec at each end of every row as follows: 4 sts once, 2 sts twice, 1 st 5 times = 73 [81] sts. Continue working

straight until work measures 56 [57]cm, 22 [22½]in. Shape shoulders by dec at each end of every row as follows: 5 sts 3 [1] times, 6 sts 2 [4] times, 19 [23] sts rem for neck.
Left front: Make 47 [51] ch in light grey and work in crochet patt, shaping armhole as for back. When work measures 27cm (10½in), shape front slope by dec 1 st at front edge on next row, then dec 1 st at same edge on every 4th row 10 [12] times. When work measures 54 [55]cm, 21¼ [21¾]in, shape shoulder by dec at armhole edge on every row as follows: 4 sts twice, 5 sts 3 times [5 sts 5 times].
Right front: Work to match left front.
Left sleeve: With No 3½mm knitting needles, cast on 54 [58] sts in dark grey and work in K1, P1 rib for 8cm (3¼in). Change to No 4 needles and work in st st, inc 1 st at each end of every 8th row 13 times = 80 [84] sts. Continue until work measures 50cm (19¾in). Shape top of sleeve by casting off at beg of every row as follows: 4 sts twice, 2 sts 6 [8] times. Dec 1 st at each end of every alt row 13 times, then cast off 2 sts at beg of next 6 rows = 22 sts. Now work straight at left edge, but at right edge cast off 4 sts at beg of next row = 18 sts. Continue working straight until work measures 78 [79]cm, 30¾ [31]in. Cast off at left edge on every alt row 9 sts once, 3 sts 3 times.
Right sleeve: Work to match left sleeve.
Welt and front band: With No 3½mm needles, cast on for entire welt 213 [229] sts in dark grey and work in K1, P1 rib, slipping first st on every row. When work measures 3cm (1¼in) work 1st buttonhole by casting off 7th–9th sts from left-hand edge, then casting on 3 sts on return row. When work measures 6cm (2¼in) rib 13 sts, cast off 187 [203] sts, rib to end. Continue working 2 sets of 13 sts for front band in K1, P1 rib, slipping first st on every row; at the same time working 3 more buttonholes on left front band at intervals of 10cm (4in). When work measures 76 [78]cm, 30¼ [30¾]in from beg, cast off.

Making up:
See page 7 for pressing and joining seams. Join seams. Join bands at back of neck and stitch band and welt to crochet pattern pieces. Sew on buttons.

GREEN JACKET
Materials:
300 [400]g yarn in dark green, 250 [300]g each in medium green and light green; 6 buttons.

Main pattern:
Multiples of 8+3.
1st row (wrong side), light green: 1 turning ch, 1 dc into 2nd st from hook, *1 ch, miss 1 st, 1 dc into next st, rep from *.
2nd row (right side), medium green: 2 turning ch, *1 tr *behind* work into the empty st of foundation chain, 1 ch, 1 tr *in front* of work into next empty st of foundation chain, 1 ch, rep from *. At end of row work 1 tr *behind* work into the last empty st of foundation ch, 1 ch, leave loop hanging free.
3rd row (right side), light green: insert hook into light-green loop of row lying below, make 4 turning ch, *twice alt 1 tr *in front* of work into foll dc of 1st row and 1 ch, then twice

alt 1 tr *behind* work into next dc and 1 ch, rep from *. At end of row work twice alt 1 tr *in front* of work into dc and 1 ch, then 1 tr *behind* work into last dc, working tog with green loop.

4th row (wrong side), medium green: as for 2nd row, but working tr into green tr sts.

5th row (wrong side), light green: as for 3rd row, working tr into light green tr sts. Rep rows 2–5.

Working instructions:

Back: Make 99 [107] ch in light green and work in crochet patt, shaping as described for grey jacket.

Left front: Make 47 [51] ch in light green and work in patt, shaping armhole as for back. When work measures 49 [50] cm, 19½ [19¾]in, dec at front edge on every row as follows: 2 sts 2 [3] times, 1 st 4 times, then on every alt row dec 1 st 3 times. Work 2 rows, then shape shoulder as described for grey jacket.

Right front: Work to match left front.

Sleeves: Work in dark green as described for sleeves of grey jacket.

Welt: With No 3½mm needles, cast on 193 [209] sts in dark green and work for 6cm (2½in) in K1, P1 rib. Cast off.

Neckband: With No 3½mm needles, cast on 85 [93] sts and work for 4cm (1½in) in K1, P1 rib. Cast off.

Front bands: With No 3½mm needles, cast on 127 [129] sts in dark green and work in K1, P1 rib, slipping first st of every row. When work measures 2cm (1in), work buttonholes by casting off 3 sts and casting on 3 on return row: work 1st buttonhole 2cm (1in) from left bottom edge and 5 more at intervals of 9cm (3½in). When work measures 4cm (1½in), cast off. Work 2nd front edging to match, without buttonholes.

Making up:

See page 7 for pressing and joining seams. Join seams. Stitch welt and neckband in place, then stitch front bands in place. Sew on buttons.

Summer cool

The lacy design of this pullover is crocheted in trebles and chain stitch. It is the ideal sweater to wear on a cool spring or summer evening.

Sizes:
To fit bust 86–91cm and 97–102cm (34–36in and 38–40in). Figures in square brackets [ ] refer to second size.

Materials:
Standard 3 ply yarn; 250 [300]g. 1 crochet hook No 2.50mm (UK size 12).

Main pattern:
See patt chart. Blank squares = 1 tr and 1 ch on odd rows and 1 ch and 1 tr on even rows, worked alternately. Coloured squares = 2 tr. Each row begins after making 2 turning ch; work begins in 2nd st and ends in top of turning ch.

Welt, neckband and cuff pattern:
Dc, beginning with wrong-side row. Each row begins after 2 turning ch; work begins in 2nd st and ends in top of turning ch.

Tension:
28 sts and 14 rows = 10cm (4in).

Working instructions:
Back: Make 143 [153] ch + 1 turning ch. Work for 3cm (1in) in dc welt patt.
Continue in main patt as shown on chart, beg with 9th square. When work measures 5cm (2in), dec 1 st at each end of next row, then 1 st at each end of every 4th row 5 times = 131 [141] sts. Now inc 1 st at each end of every 8th row 3 times = 137 [147] sts.
When work measures 40cm (15¾in), shape armholes as follows: dec 3 sts at each end of next 2 rows, 2 sts at each end of next 3 rows, 1 st at each end of next 2 rows = 109 [119] sts.
Continue in patt from chart until work measures 60 [61]cm, 23½ [24]in. Leaving centre 47 sts unworked for back of neck, shape shoulders and neck: dec on both sides 8 sts once, 9 sts twice [10 sts twice, 11 sts once]; at the same time dec at neck edge on every row, 2 sts twice, 1 st once.
Front: Work as for back up to V neck, then continue in patt and, when work measures 40 [41]cm, 15¾ [16]in, divide, leaving centre stitch unworked.
Work on each group of sts as follows: shape armhole and shoulders as on back; at the same time dec at neck edge on every row 2 sts 7 times, 1 st 8 times, then dec 1 st on every alt row 6 times.
Sleeves: Make 75 ch + 1 turning ch, work 3cm (1in) in dc. Continue in main patt from chart, beg with 8th square of patt rep. Inc 1 st at each end of every 4th row 13 times [inc 1 st at each end of every 2nd and 4th rows alt 16 times] = 101 [107] sts. Work till sleeve measures 43 [44]cm, 17 [17½]in.
Shape top of sleeve as follows: dec 5 [7] sts at each end of next row, then dec 3 sts at each end of next 3 rows, 2 sts at

each end of next 3 rows, 1 st at each end of next 4 rows, 2 sts at each end of next 3 rows, 3 sts at each end of next 3 rows, then 5 [6] sts once. 13 [13] sts rem. Fasten off.

Making up:
See page 7 for pressing and joining seams. Join seams. Starting at V of neck, work neckband as follows: 65 dc up each side of neck and 57 dc at back of neck = 187 dc. Work straight in welt patt for 3cm (1in), then stitch narrow ends of neckband together neatly at front, right over left.

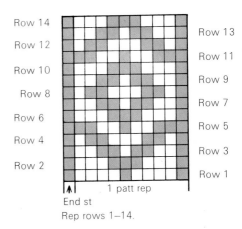

Row 14   Row 13
Row 12   Row 11
Row 10   Row 9
Row 8   Row 7
Row 6   Row 5
Row 4   Row 3
Row 2   Row 1

1 patt rep

End st

Rep rows 1–14.

Key: Blank squares = 1 tr and 1 ch.
Coloured squares = 2 tr.

Crochet and knitting for the home

Curtains like Granny's

Curtains in delicate white crochet conjure up pictures of homely comfort, reminding us of the good old days. These curtains are not difficult to make, as the squares are worked individually. Crochet them at odd moments and stitch them together to complete the picture.

Size:
Each curtain is 84cm (33in) wide and 140cm (55in) long.

Materials:
450g 2 ply cotton yarn; crochet hook No 2.50mm (UK size 12).

Tension:
1 square measures 14cm (5½in) along each side.

Design (see chart):
Make 8 ch, join into a ring with sl st.
1st round (forward round): 1 ch, *1 dc into foll st, 5 ch, miss 1 st, rep from * twice, then 1 dc into foll st, 2 ch and 1 tr into 1st dc for last corner arch.
2nd round (return round): 1 turning ch, 1 dc into short ch arch, *5 tr into dc, 1 dc into foll corner arch, 5 ch for corner, 1 dc into same arch, rep from *, then 5 tr into last dc, 1 dc into tr, 2 ch and 1 tr into 1st dc.
Continue working from chart, working end of every round as in 1st and 2nd rounds.

Border (see chart):
Start next to a corner and rep rows 2–7 until the next corner is reached, measuring strip against main work; work rows 8–15 for corner, then rep from 2nd row again and so on all the way round ending with a 7th row.

Working Instructions:
For each curtain, work 60 squares and sew together 6 squares wide and 10 squares long so that front parts of stitches are visible. Finally work border and sew on in the same way. Pin out curtains, dampen slightly and leave to dry before hanging.

Detail of one corner of square and border.

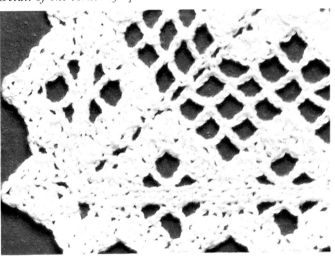

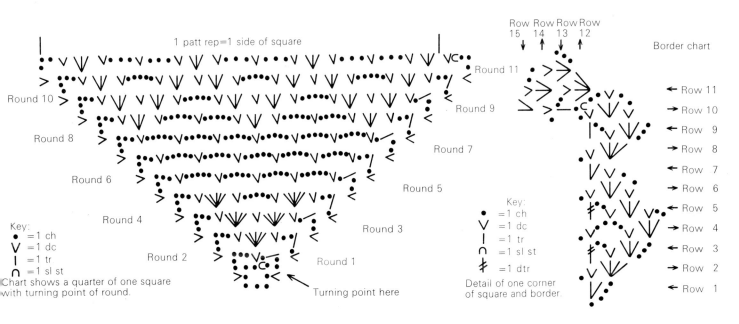

1 patt rep=1 side of square

Border chart

Round 11

Round 10

Round 9

Round 8

Round 7

Round 6

Round 5

Round 4

Round 3

Round 2

Round 1

Turning point here

Row 15 Row 14 Row 13 Row 12

← Row 11
→ Row 10
← Row 9
→ Row 8
← Row 7
→ Row 6
← Row 5
→ Row 4
← Row 3
→ Row 2
← Row 1

Key:
• =1 ch
V =1 dc
| =1 tr
∩ =1 sl st
Chart shows a quarter of one square with turning point of round.

Key:
• =1 ch
V =1 dc
| =1 tr
∩ =1 sl st
‡ =1 dtr
Detail of one corner of square and border.

Old-world charm

This bedspread is made of squares worked in many different colours. Start at the centre of each square and work outwards, using chain and treble stitches.

Size:
145cm (57in) wide by 200cm (78¾in) long.

Materials:
Standard 4 ply yarn. 1800g in white, 50g each in 15 assorted colours. Crochet hook No 3.00mm (UK size 11).

Tension:
1 square = 11cm (4½in) along each side.

Square:
Make 6 ch in white, close into a ring with sl st.
Work in rounds: *1st round:* work 12 dc into ring.
2nd round: make 3 ch for 1st tr, 1 tr into 1st st, continue working 2 tr into every st = 24 sts. End this and every foll round with 1 sl st into top of starting ch. When changing colour work sl st in the new colour.
3rd round, in colour: make 4 ch for 1st dtr, 2 dtr into next st, then work alt 1 dtr into 1 st and 2 dtr into next st = 36 sts.
4th round, in white: make 3 ch for 1st tr, 2 tr into space before 1st dtr, continue working 1 group of 3 tr after every 3 dtr. *Corner = 3 tr, 1 ch, 3 tr into same space, then work 1 group of 3 tr twice, rep from * twice, finish with 1 corner and 1 group.
5th round (worked in opposite direction) and *6th round* (worked in same direction as round 1–4), in white: work as 4th round, working groups of sts between groups and corners into corner ch spaces.

Working instructions:
The bedspread consists of 234 squares, joined in 18 rows of 13 squares each, either sewn together or joined with crochet. If using crochet to join squares, complete only the first square; leave others to be joined in the 6th round. Then in 6th round make 1 ch after 1st corner group, 1 sl st into corner ch of next square, 1 ch, then work 2nd corner group; join all other groups of tr sts in the same way, working ch between the tr groups of adjacent squares. Finally work all round the bedspread with 2 rounds of white or with coloured remnants, working 1 tr group into every space.

Edged with lace

The chunky leaf motif of this crocheted border adds a touch of rustic charm to an inviting breakfast cloth. The borders are worked sideways, repeating the motifs for length required.

Size:
Diameter of cloth=130cm (51in). Width of border=13cm (5in).

Materials:
350g cotton or synthetic yarn.
1 crochet hook No 2.00mm (UK size 11). Cotton fabric for cloth: 1.35m (1½yd) of white fabric 140cm (54in) wide.

Pattern:
Work crochet leaf border from chart, rep rows 3–10. See also detail photographs for working leaf edging.

Tension:
1 patt rep measures 8.5cm (3¼in) deep.

Working instructions:
Straight edging (border next to edge of fabric): Make 7 ch+2 turning ch.

1st row: 1 tr into 3rd ch from hook (1 ch, miss 1 ch, 1 tr into next ch) twice, 1 ch, miss 1 ch, tr into last ch, turn with 2 ch.
2nd row: 1 tr into 1st tr, (1 ch, 1 tr into next tr) twice, 1 ch, 1 tr into last tr, turn with 2 ch.
Rep 2nd row until strip length fits around edge of cloth.
Border with leaf edging: Make 19 ch+4 turning ch and work as shown on chart.
For tablecloth with a diameter of 130cm (51in), work 48 patt rep, ending last rep with an 8th row.

Leaf edging:
The following photographs show you how to work the leaves and the curve of the border itself.
1 Leaves are worked in 2 stages. First work the arches in tr and ch st: at end of 1st return row work as follows into 1st st of foundation chain: 1 tr, (3 ch, 1 tr) 3 times; on all foll return rows work this group of sts into 3rd tr of centre leaf.
2 In foll forward row of work, crochet leaves: 1 turning ch, then *1 dc, 5 tr, 1 dc, rep from * twice.
3 For the curve of the border: on every row work into 4th tr before inside edge, 1 tr, 1 ch, 1 tr.

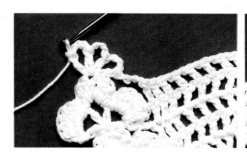

1   2   3

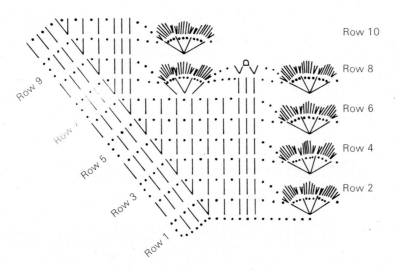

Row 10

Row 8

Row 6

Row 4

Row 2

Row 9
Row 7
Row 5
Row 3
Row 1

Key:
Chart shows 1 patt rep.
Rep rows 3–10.

● =1 ch
V =1 dc
| =1 tr
◻ =1 picot (=4 ch, 1 dc into st lying below st being worked).

Cottage setting

There is an old-world charm about this bedspread, made of separately knitted squares. You can work it to any size you like. Yarn is wound twice round the needle to form the holes in the lacy pattern. Every square has a garter stitch border.

Size:
180 × 240cm (70 × 94in).

Materials:
1950g standard 4 ply yarn in white. 5 double-pointed needles No 3½mm (UK size 9); 1 crochet hook No 3.50mm (UK size 9).

Pattern:
See chart. *1st round:* With crochet hook make 8 ch and close into a circle with a sl st. With set of needles and spare needle, knit up 1 st from each ch, winding yarn round needle *twice* between K sts = 4 sts on each needle.
2nd round: *K1 = corner st, yrn twice, K3, yrn twice, rep from * 3 times. When working double yrn from previous round, K into 1st strand and slip 2nd strand off needle, thus making a long st. Continue working from chart.

Pattern chart:
Shows 1 patt rep = ¼ of square patt. Rep patt 3 times. Chart shows all even rows: on odd rows K sts and work double yrn as described above.

Tension:
Side of square measures about 20cm (8in).

Working instructions:
Work 108 squares. See page 7 for pressing and joining seams. Sew together with 12 squares along long sides and 9 squares along shorter sides, using a flat seam so that the fronts of the stitches are visible.

Key:
× = K1
• = P1
∪ = yrn twice
╱ = K2 tog
╲ = K2 tog through back loops
↑ = slip 1, K2 tog, psso

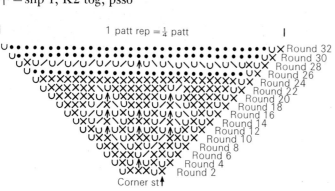

Elegant bedspread

This big, beautiful bedspread is made of white, easy-care synthetic yarn, worked in treble and chain stitch in strips. When the strips are sewn together you see the entire bold pattern. The border is worked separately and sewn on; double crochet is worked round the zig-zag edge.

Size:
235 × 150cm (92½ × 59in).

Materials:
1600g 4 ply, synthetic yarn in white. 1 crochet hook 3.50mm (UK size 9).

Chart:
Gives ½ pattern strip, plus centre square and side square, and pattern for border. Rep rows 1–28.

Tension:
19 sts and 9.5 rows = 10cm (4in).

Working instructions:
Pattern strip: For strip 28 squares of chart wide, make 57 ch + 3 turning ch and work from chart = 27 squares for the strip + 1 square (worked solid) *only* at right-hand edge. Work rows 1–28 7 times in all, then work 1 row in tr. Crochet 3 patt strips in this way; work 4th strip with 2 more sts so that there is a square worked solid at *both* sides.
Border: Starting at one corner, for border 13 squares wide,

make 27 ch + 4 turning ch, and work as shown in chart, rep rows 1–28. At right-hand edge dec 1 square on each row from rows 2–7, inc 1 square on each row from rows 9–14, continue rep patt from chart. Work corner as follows on long sides after 7 patt reps, on short sides after 4 patt reps: work rows 1–7 from chart, then finish patt as in rows 8–14 but at the same time continue dec at right-hand edge until all sts are gone. Now turn work and begin next side with row 1 from chart on left-hand side of last 13 rows. Finally sew foundation ch to left-hand side of last 13 rows.

Making up:
Oversew the pattern strips together, then sew on the border. Finally work dc all round the bedspread: 3 dc round each tr of border and turning ch, 1 dc into inside corners, 2 dc, 2 ch and 2 dc into outer points.

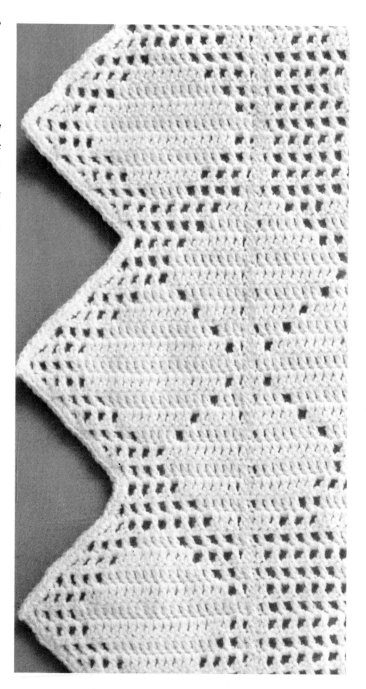

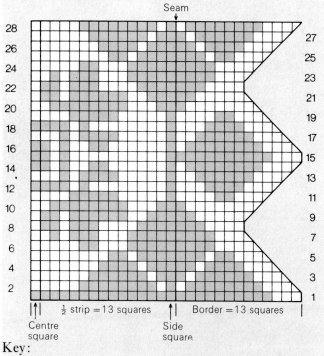

½ strip = 13 squares   Border = 13 squares
Centre square   Side square

Key:
Blank squares = alternately 1 tr and 1 ch on odd rows, and 1 ch and 1 tr on even rows.   Coloured squares = 2 tr.
Pattern strip and border are divided by seam line and are worked separately.

Different patterns from the basic triangles.

Working with cork

Coffee time

Cork is a natural plant tissue which grows on the bark of certain tree trunks and roots. Cork from the cork oak is the kind most used for technical purposes. It grows in Portugal, Spain, Algeria, France and Sicily. Cork is resilient and flexible, and makes an excellent insulating material against heat or noise.

This attractive natural material, like wood, has a grain of fine regular markings or a flecked pattern on its surface; colour varies from light to dark brown. Sheets of cork can be obtained in different sizes and thicknesses from do-it-yourself shops or dealers in building materials. At one time kitchen tables often had cork surfaces; they were easy to clean, resilient, and relatively tough, and presented a light-coloured, fine-grained appearance.

Cork has come back on the market again during the last few years. It can be used to cover walls, ceilings or floors; it is tough, and a good insulating material.

But you can make smaller and very attractive objects with cork, too. If you want to try your hand, start by using small sheets of cork. You can cut out a pattern, fit it together and glue it in place. This gives a mosaic effect. Triangles, which can be combined in many different ways, are very good for creating mosaic patterns. Here are instructions for making a tray surface of cork triangles. The triangles can be fitted together in various colour combinations, but the contrast of light and dark brown is always effective. Plain wooden trays can be obtained from any big store and given a decorative surface by this method.

1 Materials:

For a tray with interior surface measuring 40×60 cm (16×24 in) use 3 light and 3 dark cork sheets, 23×23 cm (9×9 in) and 3.2 mm thick. Adhesive (either emulsion adhesive or wood cement). A sharp knife to cut the cork; the type with a replaceable blade is best. A steel ruler and 2 sheets of sandpaper, 1 medium and 1 fine, to smooth the cut edges.

2 Cutting:

Lay cork sheets on a firm surface. Draw 10 cm (4 in) squares and divide accurately into triangles, using pencil and ruler. Cut lines neatly along edge of steel rule or ruler with a steel edge. Use a sharp blade. The blade must be drawn several times through the cork, so press hard. The grain of the cork can vary in toughness and the edges must be cut as straight as possible; it is essential to draw and cut triangles exactly in order to achieve a perfect fit.

3 Smoothing the edges:

Any slight errors and rough edges can be smoothed away with sandpaper as follows: lay a sheet of sandpaper flat and hold down with pins or drawing pins. Gather 8 to 10 triangles to form a triangular block and rub edges back and forth over the sandpaper; do not let the triangles slip apart from each other as you work.

4 Gluing in place:

Like all wood products, cork is easy to stick into place. Use emulsion adhesive such as tiling adhesive or wood cement, which can be slightly thinned with water and painted on with a flat brush. Do not paint over the whole surface of the tray with adhesive all at one time.

5 Fitting in place:

Now fit the triangles carefully into place, piece by piece to form design, and press down so that the shapes lie flat. If any adhesive is pushed up through the joins, wipe it away at once with a damp cloth. When the design is completed, test that all the triangles are firmly pressed in place. The cork surface can be finished by painting with sealer and clear lacquer.

1

2

3

4

5

Working with wood
Modern setting

This set of table mats and the table runner are made of veneer strips in natural pine. The strips are cut from veneering 1mm thick. We chose pine because the light wood, with its striking red-brown grain, goes well in a natural pine kitchen, a modern kitchen with coloured units, or a farmhouse-style kitchen, but any suitable wood or other material can be used. The woven mats are lightweight, but firm and tough, and can just be wiped clean.

Measurements:
Finished mats: approximately 42 × 36cm (16½ × 14in).
Runner: approximately 72 × 36cm (28 × 14in).
Slats for frames: 5mm (just under ¼in) thick and 2cm (¾in) wide in pine.

1 Materials:
Pine veneer strips 1mm thick and 11cm (4¼in) wide; plastic wood; pine slats for frames 0.5 × 2cm (just under ¼ × ¾in); short brass tacks 0.6cm (¼in) long; clear lacquer.

2 Cutting:
Mat: cut 6 strips 5.5 × 36cm (just over 2 × 14in) and 7 strips 5.5 × 42cm (just over 2 × 16½in). *Slats for frames:* cut 2 slats 33.5cm (just over 13in) long and 2 slats 43cm (17in) long.
Runner: cut 12 strips 5.5 × 72cm (just over 2 × 28in) and 6 strips 5.5 × 36cm (just over 2 × 14in). *Slats for frames:* cut 2 slats 70cm (27½in) long and 2 slats 33.5cm (just over 13in) long. Be careful when cutting to avoid splitting the thin wood: use a sharp knife to cut strips accurately along edge of a steel rule.

3 Smoothing:
Any rough or uneven edges are smoothed with fine sandpaper. Always rub lengthwise along the strips.

4 Weaving:
Collect strips for each mat together, 6 across and 7 up. Beginning at one corner, lay one short and one long strip across each other at right angles as shown, leaving a bare 1cm (just under ½in) free at edge. Place next strip underneath the work, hold firmly in place, insert next strip under it at a right angle. Continue weaving in this way, alternating long and short strips, and pushing work together as firmly as possible.

5 Gluing:
Tight plaiting will leave very small square holes at the points where 4 strips meet. The side strips and all the ends lying across them are glued together. Carefully raise the ends and apply adhesive with a flat brush. Lay weaving flat, cover, and weight down (e.g. with heavy books). Leave until adhesive is dry.

6 Frames:
Slats for the frames can be obtained cut to measure from do-it-yourself shops, or cut them by hand with a fine saw. Longer slats run all along the long sides of the mats, with shorter slats set between them at right angles as illustrated. Lay flat, glue together at corners and leave to dry.

7 Tacking frames in place:
Frames extend about 5mm (just under ¼in) beyond the ends of the woven strips. Using small, thin tacks, nail woven strips to frames – one tack every other strip.

8 Lacquering:
Paint over woven strips and frames on both sides with clear lacquer, to protect the light-coloured surface from dirt and make it easy to wipe clean. Using a flat brush, paint evenly in long strokes.

1

2

3

4

5

6

7

8

Dressmaking

In the peasant style

These two skirts are just the thing for a comfortable evening at home. They are long and full, and look their best in pretty flower-patterned fabrics.

The first skirt, with its delicate print of roses, has four panels and is cut very full. Gathered into the waistband, it has pockets in the side seams, and a wide frill with a gathered edge. A zip is set in at the back. A tie belt can also be added.

The second skirt, with flowers on a dark background, is cut in the same way, but without the frill. Both skirts are quick and simple to make. You can wear them with blouses or sweaters and complete the look with thick, plain-coloured stockings. These skirts can be made to fit any size; all that is needed is the waistband measurement and the skirt length. Here waist 72cm (28in) has been used as an example.

Measurements:

How to work out the width of the skirt panels: waistband measurement = 72cm (28½in) × 3 = 216cm (85½in). Using fabric 90cm (36in) wide, 4 widths are needed for the panels, which are joined by centre and side seams and remainder is used for the frill, pockets and waistband. Adjust width of panels to your own size and fabric.

Materials:

Frilled skirt: 4.10m (4½yd) of fabric 90cm (36in) wide.
Plain skirt: 3m (3½yd) of fabric 90cm (36in) wide.
For both models: 18cm (7in) zip fastener, 1 skirt hook, interlining or iron-on adhesive interfacing for waistband.

FRILLED SKIRT

Cutting out:

Skirt pattern pieces (see plan and cutting layout): cut 4 with 1cm (just under ½in) seam allowance at waist and at join with frill, and 2cm (¾in) seam allowance at sides.
Waistband: cut 1 each in fabric and interfacing; at short side of waistband add 2cm (¾in) overlap, double width, plus 1cm (just under ½in) seam allowance all round.
Pocket: cut 4 pieces with 1cm (just under ½in) seam allowance.
Frill: multiply entire width of skirt by 3: 216cm (85in) × 3 = 648cm (255in). Using fabric 90cm (36in) wide, cut frill 7 times, plus 1 piece 32cm (12½in) long; 3cm (1in) seam allowance at hem, 1cm (just under ½in) seam allowance for rest of frill.
If you want to add a tie belt, entire length of belt is about 2.50m (98in) and width 5cm (2in). Cut strip of fabric 1.70m (67in) long and another 85cm (33½in) long, both 10cm (4in) wide, plus 1cm (just under ½in) seam allowance all round.

Making up:

Trim raw edges of skirt pieces up to the waist; trim straight edges of pockets.
Close side seams, omitting slits for pockets. Stitch pocket pieces to skirt pieces, right sides together, as marked in pattern, matching to markings for slits; press upper pocket piece to front skirt piece, turn in and stitch close to edge. Press lower pocket piece away from skirt. Finally, stitch pocket pieces together round the curved side, right sides together, and trim the seam.
Close centre seams, leaving opening for zip in back centre seam. Gather skirt pieces at waist to fit waist measurement (do not use one continuous thread, as this breaks too easily). If you seem to have more fullness than you want, adjust width of skirt now at centre back and front.
Insert zip on both sides of opening. Join interfacing to waistband and stitch to skirt, finishing overlap and sewing loops for hanging skirt into side seams at the same time.

Sew frill to outside of skirt, with a gathered edge 3cm (1in) deep at the top. (If you have altered the fullness of the skirt, you must also adjust the frill to match.) Trim short sides and join to form a round. Trim long sides. Run in gathering threads. Turn in top edge 1cm (just under ½in) and press, then stitch. Do the same at the hem. Gather to same width as skirt at top edge (again, do not use one continuous thread). Now stitch frill to skirt, wrong side of frill to right side of skirt. Remove gathering threads. Finally sew on skirt hook.

Tie belt (if required): Turn under and press seam allowances all round belt pieces, place edges together and stitch through close to edge.

PLAIN SKIRT

Work this skirt in the same way as frilled skirt, but omitting the frill; instead, allow 4cm (1½in) seam allowance at hem, turn under and stitch hem. Cut tie belt in one strip (see cutting layout).

Using fabric 90cm (36in) wide, cut both models according to the cutting layouts below (frilled skirt below left, plain skirt below right). Tie-belt pattern plans have broken lines.

Pattern plans for both skirts, ready to be scaled up. Measurements are in centimetres; dotted rectangles are given for guidance in cutting out the pockets.

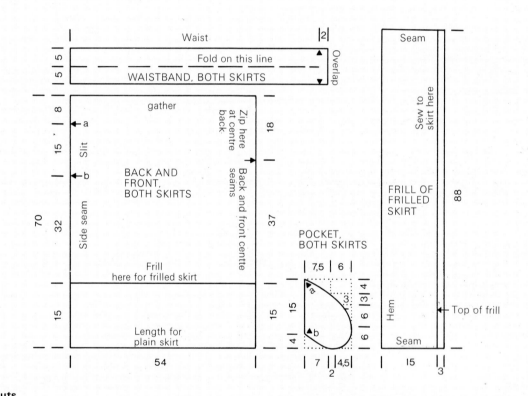

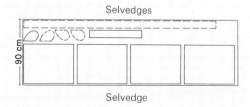

Cutting layouts

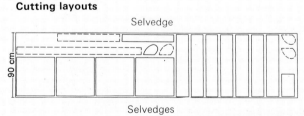

Poppet's pinafore

When baby is starting to feed herself, you can do with dozens of cover-ups like this; they are bound to get dirty, but they protect her clothes. The original pinafore was made in strong cotton but a practical alternative would be lightweight towelling, that doesn't need ironing. This pinafore fits children from 10 months.

Materials:
Remnants of cotton cord fabric for pinafore and pocket, 90cm (36in), 1.10m (44in) bias binding for trimming; length of drawstring cord.

Cutting out:
See instructions for scaling up pattern plan on page 9.
With fabric double, lay pattern pieces for pinafore and pocket against the fold and cut 1 each. Seam allowances: 4cm (1½in) at neck edge and hem, 2cm (¾in) along the back edge. 2cm (¾in) at top of pocket, otherwise no seam allowance for pocket.

Making up:
Turn under back edges of pinafore and hem. Turn seam allowances at neck edge and hem to back of work; press.At top of neck edge, stitch through once again 1cm (just under ½in) from the edge to make threading for cord.
Now cut out armholes and bind with bias binding.
Turn over seam allowance at top of pocket, press and stitch. Bind curved edge. Now stitch pocket in place as indicated in plan. Finally thread cord through neck edge and knot ends.

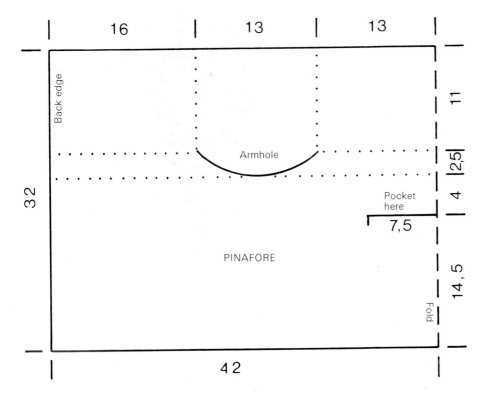

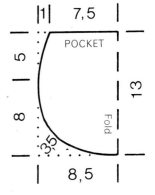

Plan of pattern pieces for the pinafore. Enlarge them to make paper pattern pieces. Measurements are in centimetres; dotted lines are for guidance.

Baby's boutique

On these pages we show you six attractive items for the nursery set. They are all easy to make, and would make acceptable gifts. Original fabrics are quoted, but make your own choice from the many suitable alternative fabrics available.

1 Dungarees in fine, spotted needlecord. A tie-belt at the waist adjusts the width. We trimmed the dungarees with a motif sewn on the front. Straps crossed over the back are fastened with press studs.

2 All-in-one romper suit in soft, pure white stretch cotton towelling. The top is trimmed with brightly coloured zig-zag braid. There is a zip at the back.

3 Simply cut cape for bath-time, with hood attached, made in towelling. The cape is gathered in at the neck with a cord which can be tied in a bow in front. Edges are bound with red bias binding.

4 Little pullover made in soft white stretch cotton towelling trimmed with zig-zag braid; it will pull on over the head. A small opening at the back fastens with a button.

5 Pinafore dress made of flowered brushed cotton, straps crossed at the back and buttoned in front. The skirt is gathered. There is a heart-shaped pocket in front and a zip at the back. The dress has a matching pair of plastic-lined pants to cover a nappy, closed with press studs at the sides. A matching head-scarf with a ruched edge completes the set.

6 All-in-one suit made in striped knitted fabric; very soft and stretchy. There is a zip at the back. It has a small matching cap with a turned-up brim.

1 DUNGAREES
Materials:
Needlecord. 2 press studs. 1.50m (60in) coloured tape.

Cutting out:
See pattern layout and instructions for scaling up on page 9. With fabric double, lay pattern pieces along fold, cut 1 of each with 3cm (1½in) seam allowance at hem, 2cm (¾in) at side seams, 4cm (1½in) at back waist, 1cm (just under ½in) at front waist, 1cm (just under ½in) at inside leg seams and round bib and facing.
Cut 1 strip of fabric 5cm (2in) wide and 32cm (12½in) long for 'tunnel' to take tape in front. Straps: cut 2 strips each 8cm (3in) wide and 28cm (11in) long.

Making up:
Stitch straps together, turn right side out (they are now 3cm (about 1in) wide). Stitch curved edge of bib to facing, turn right side out, fitting straps into place and stitching them to outer edge.
Close inside leg seams and side seams up to point marked for slit. Trim. Stitch down seam allowance along length of slit.
Stitch down a 'tunnel' 3cm (about 1in) wide along back waist. Stitch hems. Sew on 2 press studs at back waist and ends of straps. Thread 2 tapes each 75cm (30in) long through 'tunnel' at waist.

2 ROMPER SUIT

Materials:

Stretch cotton towelling. 1 zip 32cm (12in) long. Zig-zag braid, 1m (40in) each in red, yellow and blue, 40cm (16in) in green.

Cutting out:

See pattern layout and instructions for scaling up on page 9. Seam allowances: 4cm (1½in) at hem, 2cm (¾in) at back centre seam, 1cm (just under ½in) elsewhere.

Making up:

Trim all raw edges. Close shoulder seams. Stitch on braid (see picture); lowest row of braid is indicated on back and front of pattern pieces. Stitch in seam allowance at neck with the braid trimming.

Close centre back seam; set in zip. Close inside leg seams and side seams up to slit. Stitch down seam allowance at armhole.

3 TOWELLING CAPE

Materials:

Towelling fabric. 1.40m (55in) cord. 3m (10ft) of bias binding 20mm wide, 90cm (36in) of binding 30mm wide.

Cutting out:

See pattern layout and instructions for scaling up on page 9. Cut along fold of fabric with 2cm (¾in) seam allowance at hood seam, no seam allowance elsewhere.

Close hood seam, turning under 1cm (just under ½in) of seam allowance to hide raw edges; stitch through close to edge. Bind round all edges to a depth of 5mm (just under ¼in). With the 30mm-wide bias binding stitch a tunnel on cape at neck, thread cord through.

4 STRETCH TOWELLING PULLOVER:

Materials:

Stretch cotton towelling. Zig-zag braid, 1.30m (50in) each in red, yellow and blue, 40cm (16in) in green. 1 button.

Cutting out:

See pattern layout and instructions for scaling up on page 9. Cut pieces with 1cm (just under ½in) seam allowance all round.

Making up:

Trim all raw edges. Stitch braid to edges of sleeves and hem, catching in hems with bottom row of braid. Work an opening in centre of back. Catch in seam allowance at neck with braid. Sew a button and loop at sides of back opening.

5 PINAFORE DRESS, HEAD-SCARF, PANTS:

Materials:

Cotton. *Pinafore dress:* 16cm (6in) long zip, 2 buttons. *Pants:* plastic lining; 50cm (20in) of elastic 6mm (¼in) wide, 50cm (20in) of elastic 1.5cm (½in) wide, 6 press studs.

Cutting out:

See pattern layout and instructions for scaling up on page 9.

Skirt waistband: cut 1 strip 14cm (5½in) wide and 52cm (20½in) long, plus seam allowance. Skirt: cut front of skirt 20cm (8in) by 50cm (20in); cut 2 back pieces each 20cm (8in) by 25cm (10in), plus seam allowance. Straps: cut 2 strips each 8cm (3in) wide, when completed 3cm (1in), and 35cm (14in) long.

Head-scarf: draw a right angle, measure off 30cm (12in) along both sides, join ends of lines = ½ head-scarf. Leave 1cm (just under ½in) seam allowance all round. Edging strip: cut strip 5cm (2in) wide; it will be 3cm (1in) when completed; strip is 120cm (47in) long.

Pants: for layout see plan. Cut pants once in fabric and once in plastic lining material; no seam allowance for plastic lining, 3cm (1in) seam allowance at upper edge of fabric piece, elsewhere 1cm (just under ½in). Cut 2 facings (see plan) with 1cm (just under ½in) seam allowance.

Making up:

Pinafore dress: close side seams of skirt, close centre back seam leaving 13cm (5in) open at top, trim raw edges. Gather skirt into waistband and stitch. Set in zip. Stitch straps together and turn right side out, work a buttonhole 1cm (just under ½in) from the edge. Stitch straps to back of skirt 6cm (2½in) apart. Sew 2 buttons to front of skirt 10cm (4in) apart. Stitch hem.

Head-scarf: turn in one long side of the edging strip by 6mm (¼in) twice, stitch; gather the other long side to a length of 85cm (33½in) and stitch to scarf; trim seam allowances. Stitch down front edge.

Pants: baste plastic lining to fabric. Stitch sides and crotch, turn to right side, threading elastic 6mm (¼in) wide and 25cm (10in) long round each leghole as you work. Stitch down seam allowance at upper edge and thread through the wider elastic, 21cm (8½in) long at front, 23cm (9in) long at back. Sew on press studs.

6 ALL-IN-ONE SUIT, CAP

Materials:

Horizontally striped jersey. For suit: 32cm (12in) zip fastener.

Cutting out:

See pattern plan and instructions for scaling up on page 9. *Suit:* see romper suit (2), omitting braid. *Cap:* cut 1 piece along fold with 6mm (¼in) seam allowance all round.

Making up:

Suit: follow instructions for romper suit (2). *Cap:* close and trim short curved seams at top of cap. Close long seam from curve of head downwards. Turn up lower edge and stitch in place over raw edge using zig-zag stitch.

1 RED DUNGAREES

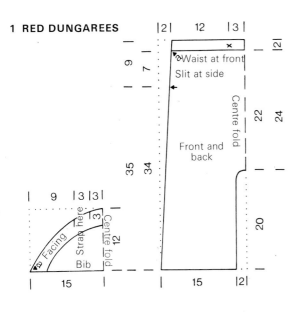

1: *Front and back of dungarees are cut the same except that back is 2cm (¾in) longer than front.*
2: *Front and back are cut the same except for the neck.*
3: *Cape and hood form one pattern piece.*
4: *Draw back and front separately then glue together at shoulder.*
5: *Draw the facing as an additional pattern piece.*
6: *Front and back of the suit are exactly the same. ½ pattern piece for the cap is shown.*

3 TOWELLING CAPE

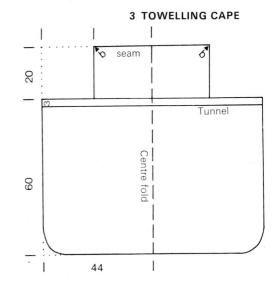

2 ROMPER SUIT

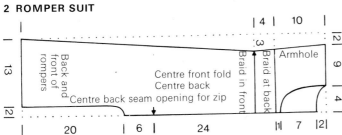

4 PULLOVER

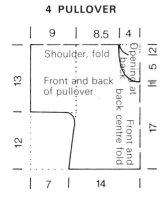

5 PLASTIC-LINED PANTS

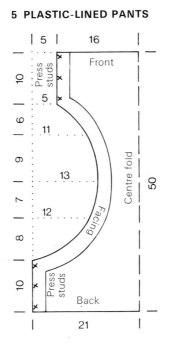

6 ALL-IN-ONE SUIT AND CAP

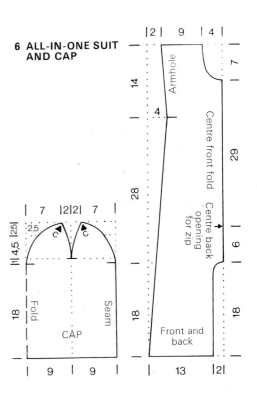

Beginner's piece

Waistcoat and skirt to run up in no time and wear with your own blouses and shirts.

Size:
Skirt and waistcoat are given in waist size 71cm (28in) and bust 86cm (34in).

Materials:
See pattern layout and instructions for scaling up on page 9.
Skirt: 3.20m (3½yd) of striped fabric 90cm (36in) wide. 1 zip 18cm (7in) long. 20cm (8in) of interfacing 90cm (36in) wide. 1 skirt hook.
Waistcoat: Horizontal striped fabric: 1m (1yd) of fabric 90cm (36in) wide. Plain fabric: 50cm (20in) of fabric 125cm (50in) wide.

Cutting out:
Skirt: When cutting striped material make sure that the stripes of the separate pieces will match up at the seams.
Cut front and back of skirt with a centre seam. Cut 4 pocket pieces. Cut waistband to required measurement; cut 1 waistband piece in fabric, 1 piece in interfacing.
Seam allowances: 2cm (¾in) at hem, 1.5cm (½in) at front and back centre seams, elsewhere 1cm (just under ½in)..For loops to hang up the skirt: cut 2 strips on the bias, each 2.5cm (1in) wide and 20cm (8in) long.
Waistcoat: Striped (right side) and plain (lining): with fabric double, lay back pattern piece along fold and cut 1 with 1cm (just under ½in) seam allowance. Cut 2 front pieces from single fabric with 2cm (¾in) seam allowance at shoulder seam, elsewhere 1cm (just under ½in).
Patch pockets: Cut 4 pieces with 1cm (just under ½in) seam allowance.
For the ties: Cut 4 strips 3cm (1in) wide (1cm, just under ½in, when finished) and 25cm (10in) long.

Making up:
Skirt: With right sides facing and seam allowances matching, stitch pocket pieces into sides of skirt as marked (do not stitch through seam allowance). Trim raw edge of straight side of pockets and edges of side seams together; turn in seam allowance towards pockets and press. Close side seams of skirt above and below pockets. Close curved seam of pockets and trim. Trim seam allowances of side seams above and below pockets and press.
Close centre seams of skirt, leaving opening for zip at back; press seams and trim. Set zip invisibly into back opening of skirt. Gather skirt into waistband. Join loop seams, right sides together, turn right side out, and stitch into skirt over side seams.
Waistband: Iron on interfacing. Turn under and stitch overlap at arrows and turn to right side. With right sides together, stitch one edge of waistband to skirt and press seam allowance upwards; trim raw edge of other side of waistband, turn over top of skirt and stitch invisibly on right side. Neaten edges of waistband with topstitching on right side. Turn under seam allowance at hem and stitch in place.

Finally sew skirt hook to waistband.

Waistcoat: Stitch 2 pocket pieces together for each pocket and turn right side out; finish top of pocket. Stitch other edges to waistcoat as indicated in plan.

Stitch tie pieces together and turn right side out; stitch to seam allowance in position on each front as marked in plan. Close side seams of both striped and lining fabrics of waistcoat. Now place 2 waistcoat shapes right sides together, baste and stitch together, up to shoulder seams; turn right side out. Baste shoulders, then close shoulder seams, using a lapped seam. Lay wrong sides of waistcoat and lining together (seam allowances will now be lying outwards); tuck in seam allowances and oversew invisibly together, close to the edge.

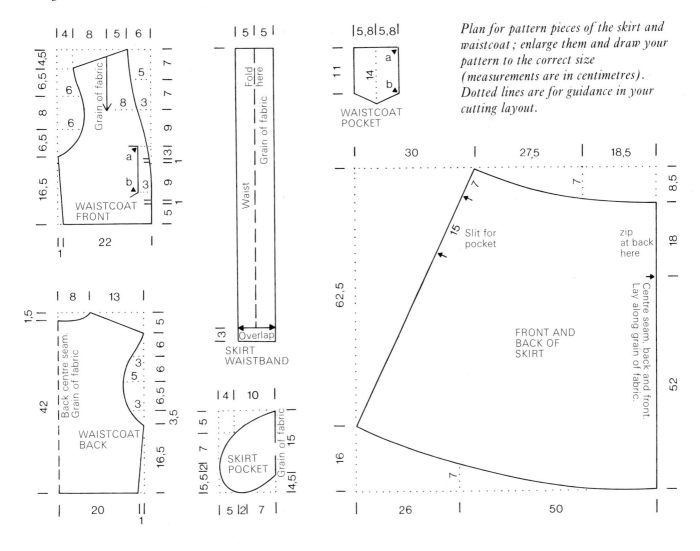

Plan for pattern pieces of the skirt and waistcoat; enlarge them and draw your pattern to the correct size (measurements are in centimetres). Dotted lines are for guidance in your cutting layout.

Casual elegance

The pattern of this overdress is simple, and it is quick to sew. The cutting out is a little tricky, since the main part of the plaid-patterned dress is cut on the bias; this is what gives it its style. The sleeves, set into a dropped shoulderline, are cut on the straight. There are pockets in the side seams. With its deep V-neck, the dress can simply be pulled on over the head, and there is room for a thick, warm sweater to be worn under it.

Material:

For size 86–91cm (34–36in) bust, 3.10m (3yd) of lightweight woollen fabric 140cm (54in) wide.

Cutting out:

Draw up and cut out a paper pattern as in plan (see instructions on page 9). Arrange pattern pieces on material as in cutting layout. Cut front and back of dress on the bias and sleeves on the straight. Cut facings for front and back of neckline as shown in plan. Cut 4 pocket pieces and cut pocket linings if necessary. *Seam allowances:* 4cm (1½in) at hem and cuffs, 2cm (¾in) at shoulder and side seams, elsewhere 1cm (just under ½in).

Making up:

When joining shoulder seams stitch in a piece of tape, otherwise the bias of fabric will pull shoulders out of shape. Trim raw edges. Join neck facing strips together at shoulder; then stitch to neckline right sides together; clip seam allowances, turn to wrong side, trim facing edge, turn hem 4cm (1½in) in from neckline and stitch.

Close side seams up to slits for pockets. Trim straight edges of pockets and stitch to slits in side seams, right sides together; turn in pockets and stitch curved pocket seams. Close sleeve seams: turn seam allowance of cuffs under twice and stitch. If using a fabric with a very obvious wrong and right side, sew on the cuff with a seam along the upper fold, so that the right side shows when it is turned up. Set sleeves into armholes, right sides together. Hang up the dress overnight before turning up the hem: trim raw edge of hem as required, turn up seam allowance, and machine-stitch in place, or stitch by hand.

Cutting layout

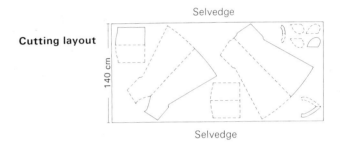

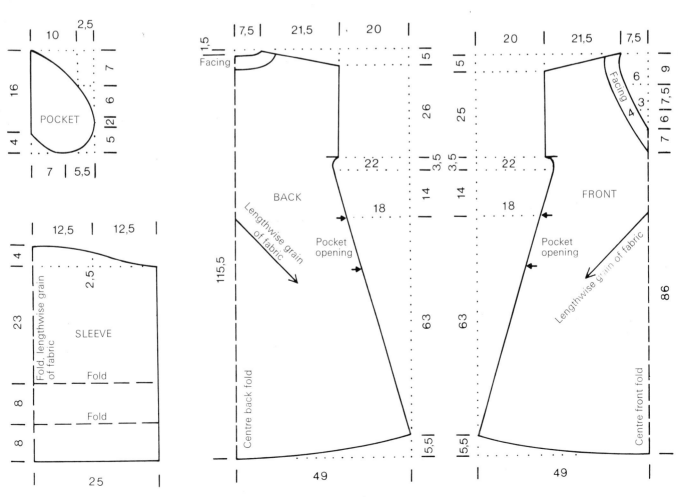

Sewing purses and bags

Bag double-up

Two shoulder-bags, one large and one small to suit your space requirements. Each bag is made of just three pieces: you can sew them up very quickly. All the edges are bound with soft leather strips and the shoulder straps are of leather too.

The plan gives pattern pieces for the bags; enlarge them to the measurements given (see page 9).

Materials:

Sailcloth: *Small bag:* 30cm (12in) of fabric 120cm (48in) wide. *Large bag:* 50cm (20in) of fabric 120cm (48in) wide. Soft leather to bind edges and for straps.

Cutting out:

Cut 1 flap, leaving 3cm (1in) seam allowance at seam joining flap to rest of bag. No seam allowance for edges to be bound with leather. Front and back of bag are the same; cut 1 of each, leaving 3cm (1in) seam allowance at top edge. Leather strap, worked double, is 3cm (1in) wide and 1m (40in) long. Pieces of leather can be joined together to make the strap; in cutting out, go by the size of leather pieces available. Edges of bag are bound with leather strips to a width of 6mm (about ¼in) on each side; here again join strips of leather, but cut them about 1.5 to 2cm (½ to ¾in) wide in the first place, to make it easier to work binding (see making up).

Making up:

Bind edges of flap, excluding seam edge: place leather strip to cover edge by 6mm (about ¼in) on right side, turn remainder over to wrong side. Gluing the leather lightly first will make the work easier. If strips have to be joined, lay start of one strip neatly over end of last one with an overlap of about 1cm (just under ½in). Stitch leather binding neatly in place; trim away surplus leather on wrong side close to seam. Now place flap and back of bag right sides together, as indicated in the plan, and stitch along marked line; trim raw edges. Then trim upper edge of front of bag. Turn in seam allowances of upper edges of front and back of bag, and stitch to edges. Now place two leather strips for shoulder strap wrong sides together and stitch. Stitch ends to back of bag to left and right of flap, stitching along existing seam line on strap. Now baste back and front of bag with wrong sides together along bottom and sides, stitch together, bind edge with leather as described above.

Measurements are given in centimetres. Dotted lines are for guidance in laying out your pattern.

Small bag

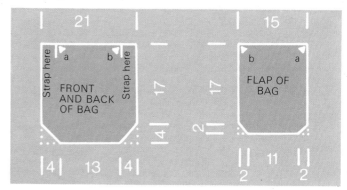

Large bag

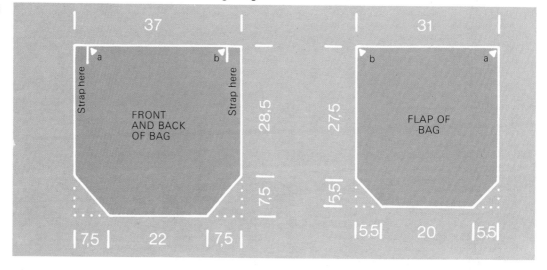

Traveller's joy

Really pretty toilet bags can be hard to find. If you have had enough of bright stripes or you don't like shiny plastic, you may have difficulty finding an alternative to suit your taste. But if you enjoy sewing, it is easy to make this bag. It would be a delightful gift, too. In fact, it is two bags in one, with an inner compartment – the ideal arrangement for taking all your toilet things when you go on a journey.

Materials:
Waterproofed or water-resistant fabric: 40cm (16in) of fabric 120cm (48in) wide. Leather for strap and 2 leather strips. 2 zip fasteners each 22cm (9in) long.

Cutting out:
See page 9 for instructions on scaling up plans.
Back and front of bag, cut in one piece: cut 2. Cut inner pocket in the same way. Leave about 6mm (just over ¼in) seam allowance all round.
Cut 1 leather strap without seam allowance.
Cut 2 leather strips with 1cm (just under ½in) seam allowance along narrow ends, no seam allowance along sides. Cut out middle section. Cut 2 strips to hold strap in place, without seam allowance.

Making up:
The toilet bag consists of two separate bags joined in the middle along the top. Sew each separately first. Inner pocket: stitch folds firmly along the lines indicated, placing x against o. Trim raw edges if necessary. Turn in seam allowance of upper edge and stitch firmly. Turn in seam allowances of sides and lower edge and stitch inner pocket to back of bag as shown in the plan. (Place stitching lines together and stitch through them.)
Now stitch leather strips (e to f) to main part of bag, as indicated in the plan, right side of bag to wrong side of leather. Then insert zip fastener under leather strip, with seam allowance of bag lying between leather strip and fabric of zip. Stitch fold at bottom of bag, so that it lies on the inside. Close side seams, right sides together (e–g and h–e) and trim seams.
Now close seams at bottom of bag from corner to corner, laying g to g and h to h. Trim seam.
Before closing short sides of bag at upper edge, clip seam allowance of front diagonally towards corners. Close and trim seams.
Now turn bag right side out.
Work second bag in the same way.
Stitch two bags together along upper edges of backs of bags. Glue the narrow strips to hold the strap over the ends of the strap, as shown in the plan. Then stitch ends all round and across strap. Hand-stitch ends of strips to point marked in the plan (i), thus forming a handle.

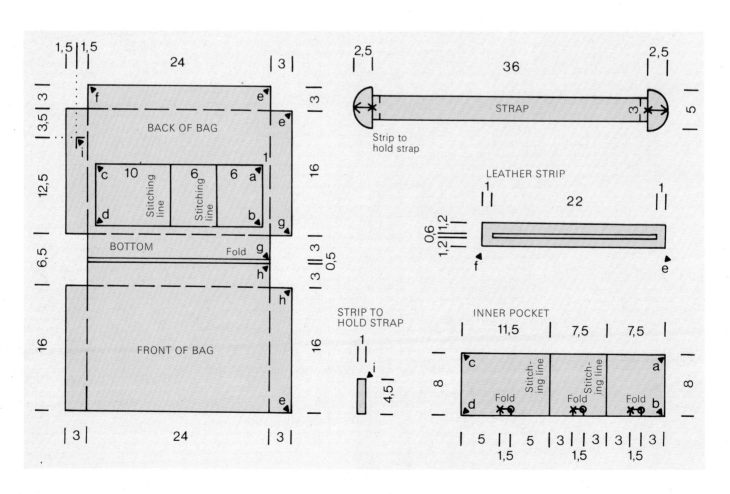

All set

This little bag is especially suitable for a make-up bag, but of course you can keep other things in it – your sewing kit, for example. It is made of sailcloth and edged with vinyl. Inside it is divided so that everything has its own place and you can find things quickly. An extra pocket inside gives even more space for odds and ends.

Materials:

50cm (20in) of sailcloth 150cm (60in) wide. (If using fabric of a different width you can easily work out the amount required for yourself.)

Vinyl: 10cm (4in) of vinyl 150cm (60in) wide. Plastic film for the 2 pockets at the top of the bag. Elastic: 25cm (10in) of elastic 2cm ($\frac{3}{4}$in) wide. 2 press studs, 1.5cm ($\frac{1}{2}$in) in diameter. 2 metal rings for the fastening, 3.5cm ($1\frac{1}{2}$in) in diameter.

Cutting out:

Cut all pieces as in plan without seam allowance except for the extra pocket pieces; extra pocket pieces, leave 2cm ($\frac{3}{4}$in) seam allowance where the edges will meet. Cut 2 top pockets from plastic film. Cut vinyl pieces as follows: strap, cut 1 piece along fold with vinyl double, leaving about 5mm (just under $\frac{1}{4}$in) seam allowance; cut 4 pieces for flaps on extra pocket without seam allowance. To bind edges, cut strips

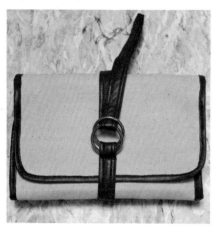

1cm (just under $\frac{1}{2}$in) wide; cut one piece 2cm ($\frac{3}{4}$in) wide by 1cm (just under $\frac{1}{2}$in) long for each end of elastic loops (4 in all). Elastic loops: 12cm ($4\frac{3}{4}$in) long.

Making up:

Bind upper edges of film pockets with vinyl strips, laying them lengthwise along the film, folding over and stitching in place. Now lay the 2 film pockets one on top of the other, with lower edges meeting. Bind lower edges together. Finally lay the 2 pockets on main part of the bag, as indicated in plan, and stitch through along bottom of the 2 pockets. Now sew on elastic loops as marked in plan, stitching the vinyl pieces over their ends; stitch through elastic as marked

on plan to make loops. Next bind edges of side flaps with vinyl and stitch to main part of bag as indicated.

Trim raw edges of extra pocket, turn in seam allowance and stitch. Place small vinyl flap pieces together in pairs, wrong sides together, and stitch. Bind flap of extra pocket. As you stitch this binding, stitch in small vinyl flaps as shown in plan. Then stitch extra pocket to main part of bag.

Now bind edges of bag, making sure the ends of the vinyl strips are neatly joined. Turn in seam allowances of strap, place edges together and stitch round strap. Put rings through strap at straight end and stitch end firmly. Stitch strap into lower stitching line of film pockets (point h). Finally punch the 2 press studs into place.

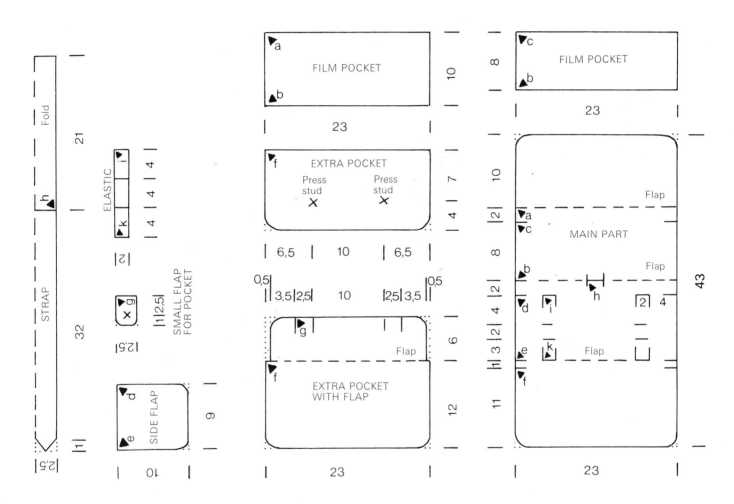

Pattern layout: enlarge pattern plans to make paper patterns and cut to the required size. Measurements are given in centimetres. Round off the corners as shown here by dotted lines.

Room for everything

Made of jute crocheted round string, with straps running from bottom to top of bag and acting as handles, this useful holdall is smart as well as practical.

Size:
55cm (21½in) wide by 40cm (15½in) deep.

Materials:
Approximately 100 metres 3 ply jute. About 40m (44yd) thick string 5mm in diameter. 1 crochet hook size 3.50mm (UK size 9).

Tension:
17 sts and 11 rounds = 10cm (4in).

Pattern:
Double crochet worked in continuous rounds, stitches worked with jute round thick string, inserting hook into backs of stitches only on previous rounds.

Working instructions:
Bag: Starting at bottom, make 24 ch + 1 turning ch.
1st round: Lay string beside foundation chain; starting in 2nd st, work 23 dc as in patt, then work 6 dc into last st, finally make 23 more ch on other side of foundation ch, 6 more dc into turning ch. Mark centre of each 6 dc group to form narrow sides of bag with a thread.
2nd round: Work in patt, working 4 dc into 2nd st at each side of marking threads.
3rd–7th rounds: As for 2nd round, but working groups of 4 dc 2 sts further away from centres on each round.
8th round: Work 2 sts into 4th st each side of centres.
9th–15th rounds: As for 8th round.
Work *16th round*, then inc as for 8th round but only on every 3rd round, working intervening rounds with no inc.
After 43 rounds cut the string, work jute over the end, work 2 sl sts, cut jute, sew end in firmly.
Strap: For finished length of 340cm (134in), cut 27m (29½yd) of jute and fold in three. Work as follows: make a loop, as for crochet, in the middle of the 27m length, place index finger of right hand through loop, holding crossed strands together with thumb and middle finger of same hand. *Now insert left index finger through loop from front to back and pull through the left-hand strand. Holding crossed strands together in left hand, remove right index finger from first loop and pull strand tight. Place right index finger through loop from front to back, pull right-hand strand through. Holding crossed strands in right hand again, remove left index finger from loop and pull strand tight. Rep from *.

Making up:
Lay the bag flat, mark 2 points 20cm (8in) apart at bottom of bag, and 4 points each 18cm (7in) away from narrow sides at top edge. Sew strap to bag over these points, joining ends of strap at base of bag and sewing firmly in place.

Sewing with remnants

pentagons from different fabric remnants; seam allowance is 1cm (just under $\frac{1}{2}$in) all round. Now sew pentagons together as follows: join 2 sets of 5 pentagons each to form a semi-circle (see plan right, pentagons 2–6 and 7–11). Now curve each semi-circle and fit together, so that the points of one part match the indentations of the other; then stitch the two parts together. Stitch in the 2 remaining pentagons (1 and 12), leaving 2 seams of one open for filling. Fill ball with stuffing material, close open seams by hand.

Patchwork playmates

These soft balls, made in pentagon shapes, cannot hurt anyone. They are filled with kapok and can be made from all sorts of coloured remnants of fabric.

FOR EACH BALL
Materials:
Remnants of fabric for 12 pentagons in all. Kapok or foam chips for the filling; amount required varies with size of ball.

Making up:
Cut cardboard template for pentagon (adjusting size to desired size of ball) as follows: first draw a circle; this is most easily done with a pair of compasses, or draw round any circular object. Measure round circumference of circle, divide equally in five parts; mark points and join them (see plan right). Cut out template. Using this template, cut 12

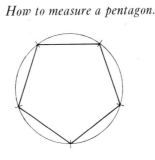

How to measure a pentagon.

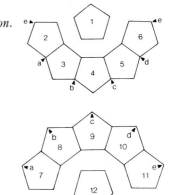

Right: arrangement of pentagons for sewing.

Strips and stripes

We made this soft, brightly coloured rug and matching cushions from remnants of plain and patterned fabric – good value for money. Try the remnants counters of your local shops and stores.

The rug has a layer of wadding inside to plump it up. It is 120cm (47in) wide and 235cm (92½in) long. However, you could work it to any size you like, but remember that the quilting effect caused by stitching through the fabric and the wadding means that the rug will lose a little of the original length.

Cushion covers can be made of remnants, or of plain fabric stitched to create the quilted effect. They too are filled with wadding.

RUG
Materials:
Surface of rug: assorted plain and patterned remnants of cotton.
Underside of rug: 2.45m (2¾yd) of plain cotton or suitable fabric 150cm (60in) wide. You will also need 4 strips of fabric to bind the edges: 2 strips 1.20m (48in) long and 2 strips 2.45m (96½in) long, each strip 8cm (3in) wide.
Wadding material: 2.45m (2¾yd) of material 150cm (60in) wide.

Working instructions:
Cut wadding and plain fabric for underside of rug to original size 243 × 120cm (96 × 47in), or as required. Sort and arrange remnants according to pattern and colour as in illustration: allow 1cm (just under ½in) seam allowance along both long sides of strips. Now stitch strips together and press seams, then place underside and surface of rug, wrong sides together, with wadding in between, and baste all three layers together with large tacking stitches. Machine-stitch through rug along strips, following lines of seams exactly.

Binding: Bind short ends first as follows: stitch a strip across one end, 3cm (1in) in from the edge, right sides together, turn strip over and fold at the edge. Turn under edge of strip for hem and sew to underside of rug. Work binding of long sides in the same way.

CUSHIONS
1 Cut 2 pieces of plain cotton fabric to the measurements shown in plan, leaving 1cm (just under ½in) seam allowance all round, and 5 pieces of wadding cut to full size of cover without seam allowance.
Place one piece of fabric over half a layer of wadding (remainder is used later to fill cushion), baste together with large tacking stitches, machine-stitch through both layers (see plan for spacing of stitching lines).
2 Cut 1 piece of plain cotton fabric for back of cushion cover and several strips for front of cushion cover, following measurements shown in plan and leaving 1cm (just under ½in) seam allowance all round. Cut 5 pieces of wadding without seam allowance.
Stitch strips of fabric together, press seams. Now place front of cushion cover over half a layer of wadding, baste together, machine-stitch through both pieces, following seam lines of joined strips.
3 Cut 1 piece each of plain (back) and patterned (front) fabric, following measurements shown in plan and leaving 1cm (just under ½in) seam allowance all round. Cut 5 pieces of wadding without seam allowance.
Place front of cushion cover over half a layer of wadding and baste together, stitch through both pieces at regular intervals (for stitching lines see plan).
4 Cut 1 piece of plain cotton fabric for back, following measurements shown in plan and leaving 1cm (just under ½in) seam allowance all round. For front of cover, cut 4 strips of plain fabric for border, each 40 × 5cm (16 × 2in) wide, leaving 1cm (just under ½in) seam allowance all round. Cut 1 square in plain contrasting fabric, and 1 patterned strip, leaving 1cm (just under ½in) seam allowance (for measurements see plan). Cut 5 pieces of wadding without seam allowance.
Now stitch together 4 strips for border at right angles to form a square. Then turn under and press seam allowance along long sides of patterned strip and stitch to the contrasting square of fabric as shown in plan. Now turn under and press seam allowances of square and stitch to border.
5 Cut 2 pieces of plain cotton fabric leaving 1cm (just under ½in) seam allowance, 5 pieces of wadding without seam allowance, following measurements shown in plan.
Place one piece of fabric on top of one layer of wadding, baste together and stitch through in squares (for stitching lines see plan).

Making up:
Join seams on cushion covers, leaving an opening for filling, and turn right side out. Fill each cover with remaining wadding and then hand-stitch opening in seam.

Plans for cushions

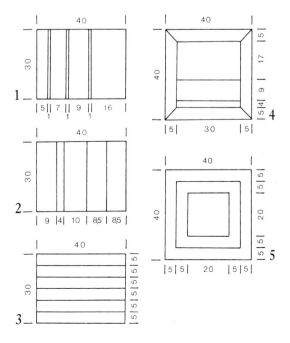

Index

Abbreviations 8
Appliqué 42–5

Bags 37–9, 56, 148–54
  all-purpose 154
  beadwork 56–7
  evening, woven 37–9
  make-up 152–3
  pendant 56
  sailcloth 148–9, 152–3
  travelling 150–1
Bangles 56
Batik 46–7
Beadwork 56–7
Bedspreads
  crochet 124, 130
  knitted 128
Belt decoration 17
Blanket, woven 40–1
Boxes, painted 12–13
Brooch, enamelled 16

Canvas-work cushions 32–6
Cork tray 132–3
Counted embroidery 9, 32–6
Crochet 110–27, 130–1
  American terminology 8
  bedspreads 124–5, 130–1
  caps 115
  curtains 122–3
  hairpin 116–17
  hook sizes, table of 8
  making up 7
  men's jackets 118–19

  notes 7
  rug 54–5
  shawl, hairpin 116–17
  tablecloth 126–7
  women's jackets 111, 112–13
  women's sweater 120–1
  women's tank top 114
  women's waistcoat 110
Cross stitch, counted 9
Cushions 32–6, 156–7

Dressmaking
  for babies 139–43
  overdress 146–7
  paper patterns for 9
  skirts 136–8, 144
  waistcoat 144–5

Embroidery 18–36
  alphabet 30–1
  counted 9, 32–6
  finishing 9
  napkins 22–3
  notes 8
  on knitting 8, 81
  tablecloths 18–19, 20–1, 24–7, 28–9
  tracing and transferring motifs 9
Enamelling 14–17

Flowers, painted 10–11

Garter stitch 8

Hairpin crochet 116–17

Jewelry 14–17, 56
  beadwork 56
  enamelling 14–17

Knitting 72–109, 128–9
  bedspread 128
  embroidery on 8
  making up 7
  needle sizes, table of 8
  notes 7
  stitches, basic 8
Knitting for children
  baby's cap 77
  baby's jumper 76
  dress 78
  jumper 72
  sweater 78
  tank tops 104–5
Knitting for men
  cardigan 85–7
  sweaters 74–5, 84, 90–1, 100–1, 106–7
  tank top 74
Knitting for women
  caps 81, 95
  cardigans 85–6, 88–9
  gloves 82
  jackets 94, 99
  jumpers 72, 76
  scarf 81
  sweaters 82–4, 88, 90–1, 92–3, 94–5, 96–7, 98, 106–9
  twin set 102–3
Making up knitted garments 7
Metrication 7

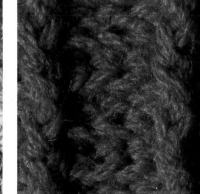

Paper patterns 9
Patchwork balls 155
Pendants 16–17
Pressing knitting 7
Puppets 68–71
Purse, belt 56–7

Reverse stocking stitch 8
Rugmaking 48–55
  crochet 54
  finishing 9
  knot, working 9
  notes 8–9
  with remnants 50–1, 156–7
  woollen 48–9, 52–3

Seam stitch 7
Soft toys 58–71
  balls 155
  bear 60–1
  cat 69
  cow 69

dachshund 69
donkey 70
elephant 62–3
hare 62
hippopotamus 64–5
lion 60
monkey, giant 66–7
paper patterns for 9
penguin 61
pig 59, 69
piglet 58
puppets 68–71
sheep 70
tortoise 64–5
Swiss darning 8

Tablecloths 18, 20, 24, 28, 126
Table settings 22–3, 132–5
  napkins 22–3
  place mats 134–5
  tray, cork 132–3
Tank tops
  child's 104
  man's 74
  woman's 114
Tension, checking 7
Tracing and transferring motifs 9

Waistcoats 110, 144
Weaving 37–41
  blanket 40
  evening bags 37–9
  frames 41
Wooden place settings 134–5

Yarn, choosing 7